Troilus and Criseyde
the poem and the frame

℘

Troilus and Criseyde
the poem and the frame

❡

Allen J. Frantzen

Twayne Publishers • New York
Maxwell Macmillan Canada • Toronto
Maxwell Macmillan International • New York Oxford Singapore Sydney

Twayne's Masterwork Studies No. 113

Copyright © 1993 by Twayne Publishers

Twayne Publishers	Maxwell Macmillan Canada, Inc.
Macmillan Publishing Company	1200 Eglinton Avenue East
866 Third Avenue	Suite 200
New York, New York 10022	Don Mills, Ontario M3C 3N1

Library of Congress Cataloging-in-Publication Data
Frantzen, Allen J., 1947–
Troilus and Criseyde : the poem and the frame / Allen J. Frantzen.
p. cm. — (Twayne's masterwork studies ; no. 113)
Includes bibliographical references and index.
ISBN 0-8057-9427-1 (cloth). — ISBN 0-8057-8581-7 (pbk.)
1. Chaucer, Geoffrey, d. 1400. Troilus and Criseyde. 2. Troilus (Legendary character) in literature. 3. Frame-stories—History and criticism. 4. Trojan War in literature. I. Title. II. Series.
PR1896. 1993
821'.1—dc20   92-39808
                                          CIP

To Waldtraut Wollburg

contents

preface

More people have lived the story of Chaucer's *Troilus and Criseyde* than have read the poem. The aristocrats of ancient Troy exist amid grand passion and myth-making calamity, but the love affair of Troilus and Criseyde follows a pattern familiar in the lesser realms of modern life. For Troilus love is serendipitous; for Criseyde it is a decision. When both embrace it, they find sexual excitement, ecstasy, and even spiritual union. Then, just as suddenly, the lovers learn that they must part, and their affair staggers to an agonizing and ambivalent close. Troilus dies a hero; he is wafted through celestial spheres toward some vague resting place for those made wise in death. Criseyde lives; more victim than victimizer, she nonetheless becomes an infamous archetype of infidelity. Beneath the grandeur of their fates is a fact that one need be no scholar to recognize: when the joy of romance begins, it is impossible to think of the end. Nevertheless, when the end arrives, one must either accept it and look ahead to new love, which is Criseyde's response, or deny it and cling to the past, the futile recourse of Troilus. As if pressed to escape these familiar and depressing alternatives, Chaucer musters the forces of piety and religion at the conclusion to insist that the only love worth having, after all, is the love of God; but his inevitable and traditional gesture is a cold proposition. Even in Chaucer's time, it could not have consoled readers who thought of the poem in terms of their own experience. If nothing is more delightful than falling in love, nothing is more painful than falling out of it. The consolations that theology and philosophy offer for such suffering hardly mitigate the intensity of the experience, much less obliterate it.

Nonetheless, one should not read *Troilus and Criseyde* as therapy for disappointment in love or for guidance in managing love affairs. The scholarly tradition surrounding the poem, ever decorous and discreet, shows that most of Chaucer's professional readers have, at least in print, kept their distance from the poem's emotional core. But academic discussions, if sometimes dry, are seldom so benighted as to insist that other subjects are more important to this text than are love and its loss. Allegorical, spiritual, and deeply moralistic readings of the poem have been produced in abundance almost from the start (and are produced today), but not all responses insist on reducing the poem's emotional, even erotic power, to a few truths about medieval life. Furthermore, the tradition has also done justice to the vigor of Chaucer's manner. If readers cannot ignore the philosophical complexity and artistic sophistication of the text, neither can they miss its humor.

Variety distinguishes Chaucer's handling of his materials, and to emphasize his presentation I use a familiar artistic device: the frame. A textual frame determines limits to a narrative exactly as a visual frame encloses a picture. History has placed many frames around *Troilus and Criseyde*, and Chaucer has placed many frames within the poem as a means of structuring his complex plot. To concentrate on the frame is not to forget the text but is rather to ask how and where we see its edges, its openings, its points of contact with the world around it and outside it. By concentrating on the frame, we connect our ways of seeing to what we see and consider, in theoretical terms, how method produces meaning.

This book is organized into four parts. Chapter 1 situates Chaucer and the story of Troy in his age. Chapter 2 discusses the importance of the text. Chapter 3 reviews the issues that have historically been significant in the reception of *Troilus and Criseyde*. Chapter 4 begins the fourth part of the book with an introduction to the frame; chapters 5 through 9 offer a reading of the poem and its framing activities, not a single literary interpretation but rather a series of related views. Chapter 10 raises some issues for further consideration. The bibliography that follows recommends several introductions to social and literary aspects of the text and to Chaucer's time.

note on the references
and acknowledgments

All quotations from Chaucer's works are taken, with permission of the publisher, from *The Riverside Chaucer*, edited by Larry D. Benson. Citations from *Troilus and Criseyde* are given by book and line number (e.g., 3.1171–74 for book 3, lines 1171–74). Citations from *The Canterbury Tales* are given by fragment number and line number (e.g., VII, 3394–97, for Fragment VII, lines 3394–97). Other poems are cited by line number only: *The Book of the Duchess* (103) for line 103 from that poem as found in *The Riverside Chaucer*.

I happily acknowledge my debt to Loyola University of Chicago for support for this project. I thank the staff of the Newberry Library, Chicago, and the Folger Shakespeare Library, Washington, D.C., for access to early editions of Chaucer's works. Karma Lochrie and Richard Rambuss commented generously on early drafts of the manuscript, and Graham D. Caie, Andrew Cole, John Flannigan, and Steven Wartofsky made helpful suggestions. Barbara Gusick ably assisted preparation of the final manuscript, and I am greatly indebted to her. Waldtraut Wollburg provided peace and quiet and good company when I wrote the final draft in Augsburg; I thank her for her many contributions to this book and to my happiness in working on it.

chronology:
Chaucer's life and works

ca. 1340   Chaucer is born in London to Agnes de Copton and John Chaucer.

ca. 1355   Serves in the court of Countess of Ulster, wife of the Duke of Clarence, second son of Edward III.

1366   Marries Philippa Roet, sister of Katherine of Swynford, who was mistress and third wife of John of Gaunt.

1367–1369   Becomes yeoman and then esquire in the household of Edward III. Writes *The Book of the Duchess* for Blanche, first wife of John of Gaunt, who died in 1368.

1370–1380?   Travels on the Continent; visits Italy.

1374–1385   Appointed controller of customs.

1378   Writes *The House of Fame*.

1381   Peasants' Rising; in London the Savoy, the palace of John of Gaunt, is burned and the Tower of London is taken.

1380–1382   Writes *The Parliament of Fowls*.

1380–1387   Translates *The Consolation of Philosophy* by Boethius; writes *Troilus and Criseyde*, "The Knight's Tale," and "Anelida and Arcite."

1385   Becomes justice of the peace for Kent and withdraws from the London royal circle.

Literary and Historical Context

❡

1

Social Text, Historical Context

Chaucer did not live in a golden age, although readers are often encouraged to think that he did. That idea, however attractive, is a form of literary history in reverse; it is the effect of a successful author's reputation on his age. The magnitude of Chaucer's achievement invites us to call forth a prodigious culture to stand behind it. But the author's glories will not suffice to dress his age as well as himself in a golden glow. Indeed, Chaucer seems to have had the same ideas about his time that many others have had about their own. Chaucer's short ballad, "Lak of Stedfastnesse," which concludes with a pointed "Lenvoy to King Richard," warns that valued institutions were collapsing and the old order decaying by the moment: the government was reckless, the Church was enslaved by corrupt clergy, merchants were unscrupulous, and laborers reluctant. "O prince," the envoy implores,

> Shew forth thy swerd of castigacioun,
> Dred God, do law, love trouthe and worthinesse,
> And wed thy folk agein to stedfastnesse.[1]

There is much evidence to confirm Chaucer's grim view of the late fourteenth century. At the century's beginning, May McKisack writes, England was "a prosperous land, a land of expanding population, flourishing agriculture, fair cities, rising universities and schools."[2] But the 40 years before Chaucer's birth c. 1340 saw increasing burdens of royal taxation to support foreign wars.[3]

During his early years the Black Death devastated the population. In the early 1380s, when Chaucer was writing *Troilus and Criseyde*, the nation was recovering from the "Peasants' Rising" of 1381, an event that signaled dissatisfaction with the structure of wages and controls on the mobility of workers. The revolt was not a local matter of peasant unrest; the demographic changes wrought by the Black Death and its aftermath affected urban and rural society.[4]

As the century ended, the government was divided in a struggle between the king and his lords. The close of the reign of Edward III (who died in 1377) was marked by waning public confidence in the executive, which was exacerbated by the ascent of a minor to the throne. Richard II, who was born in 1367 and crowned when he was merely a boy, ruled from 1377 to 1399. His reign is noted for chaos created by questionable political judgment and by an unpopular taste for displays of royal power. Some of his advisers, including Thomas Usk and Nicholas Brembre, were accused of taking advantage of the king's youth and defrauding the nation. Their executions in 1388 did not conclude the turmoil of Richard's reign. He was deposed in 1399 and replaced by Henry of Lancaster (Henry IV). Richard "rode roughshod over common right," McKisack writes, "and the nation at last repudiated him for the tyrant that he was" (McKisack, 496).

Chaucer's career unfolded in a court that witnessed sometimes violent redefinitions of power. He was one of some 40 young gentlemen in the king's employ in 1367. In the following years he traveled abroad as one of the king's envoys to France and Italy. In 1374 he was appointed controller of the customhouse in London, where he monitored export taxes on wool, the nation's most important commodity. During this period (which lasted to the mid-1380s) Chaucer also traveled as one of the king's messengers. He survived fighting between Parliament and the king that in 1388 cost Usk, Brembre, Sir Simon Burley, and Robert Tresilian their lives. In 1389 he assumed the duties of clerk of the king's works and, headquartered now in Kent, continued in royal service until his death in 1400. When Richard was deposed in 1399, Chaucer wrote a short poem with an envoy saluting Henry IV as the conqueror of "Brutes Albyon," thus seeking to have his annuity renewed under the new monarch ("The Complaint of Chaucer to His Purse," Benson, *RC*, 656). He succeeded; he was, it seems, never out of favor.

While he pursued these official occupations, Chaucer also pursued his literary career. During the period of his service at the customhouse he translated *The Consolation of Philosophy*, by Boethius, and wrote *The House of Fame*, *The Parliament of Fowls*, and *Troilus and Criseyde*.[5] Since centers of power were also centers of reading and writing—activity often referred to as "literary production"—we might expect the poet to have taken the political upheavals of these years into account. How, we might ask, did Chaucer combine the world of writing and that of his profession?

The study of Chaucer's historical context is not a simple matter of exploring the "influence" of his age or tracing poetic observations of social change. The poet's position was more complex than such analysis would allow. As esquire and royal appointee, Chaucer belonged to a new class of professional administrators, educated but not academic, whose connections to political power were the result of a combination of fortunate (but not noble) birth and professional skills. Those connections did not depend on ancient loyalties; rather, they were managed by the nobility and by those of "gentil" birth for their mutual benefit. Paul Strohm has recently proposed that we describe the poet situated in these conditions as the "social Chaucer," a writer conscious of the demands of commercial and political groups competing for influence and negotiating power amid political uncertainty. Strohm argues that Chaucer wrote at a time when "a system in which loyalties were defined vertically in terms of ties to a social superior" was becoming a network of "horizontal agreements between persons in similar social situations." This shift, he argues, took place within "the textual realm" that consists of "imaginative productions through which people become aware of conflict and fight it out." Such fictions, as Strohm points out, could represent and resolve such conflicts in multiple ways, not only those agreeable to their authors.[6]

Our understanding of "social Chaucer" benefits from another concept, that of "public poetry," Anne Middleton's term for a kind of fourteenth-century poetry concerned with social well-being. The voice of the public poet, she writes, is "pious." Its "central pieties" are "worldly felicity and peaceful, harmonious communal existence." Such felicities rest on economic foundations. The problems of labor, distribution of wealth, and integrity of government all affected the "common good" or "commun profit," Chaucer's phrase for social well-being in *The Parliament of Fowls* (47, 75, 507). But these concerns are, as Middleton observes, found in Chaucer's fiction rather than in writing directly addressed to the public.[7] Even in fiction, the poet rarely draws attention to political problems in more than a generalized—and often idealized—sense. This fact is a credit to Chaucer's tact, no doubt, but a debit to the social engagement of his work, for his appears to be a (completely?) successful attempt at obscuring the links between his position as a poet and his influence as a public servant.

While other poets assailed social injustice in vivid satire—William Langland and John Gower, for example—Chaucer virtually ignored contemporary events. There are exceptions. One is the death of Blanche, wife of John of Gaunt, who is commemorated in *The Book of the Duchess*. Another is the link of *The Parliament of Fowls* to the failed attempts to find a queen for Richard between 1377 and the date of his marriage to Anne of Bohemia in 1382.[8] To see the various possibilities for social commentary—as opposed to flattering (or gently admonishing) one's royal patrons—one has only to turn to Gower's *Vox clamantis* ("The voice of one crying"), which links the Peasants' Rising to the fate of Troy. The peasants are compared to wild beasts; they arm themselves and storm the city, as the Greeks assaulted Troy. "The peasant attacked and the knight in the city did not resist," Gower wrote. "Troy was without a Hector."[9] Troy was a popular subject in the Middle Ages, when London was seen as the "New Troy." In *The Troy Book*, Chaucer's contemporary, John Lydgate, wrote 30,000 lines on the subject; Chaucer touched on it in *The Book of the Duchess* (326–34). It also appears at the beginning of *Sir Gawain and the Green Knight* and elsewhere. But neither the commonplace linking of London with Troy nor Gower's criticism of weak government unable to control its lower classes is important in *Troilus and Criseyde*. Social criticism of any kind is, in my view, far from Chaucer's subject. Chaucer's only direct reference to the rising, for example, is this rather light-hearted aside in "The Nun's Priest's Tale"[10]:

Certes, he Jakke Straw and his meynee
Ne made nevere shoutes half so shrille
Whan that they wolden any Flemyng kille,
As thilke day was maad upon the fox. (VII, 3394–97)

When the peasants stormed London, they dragged Flemish prisoners from their jails and slaughtered them. This event, seen as nothing compared to the escape of the fox with the rooster, humorously shrinks even further in significance when compared to the catastrophes that seemingly matter so much to the Nun's Priest, including the burning of Rome, the destruction of Carthage, and the fall of Troy (VII, 3355–74).

The Parliament of Fowls is an equally revealing demonstration of Chaucer's skill at neutralizing the explosive potential of political references. This dream vision makes use of the famous Somnium Scipionis ("The dream of Scipio"), a text by Cicero about Scipio Africanus, a Roman general. The story of Scipio formed the final part of Cicero's De Re Publica ("The republic"); it involved a contest of wills between a monarch and his followers, a tension between rebellion and social order. Cicero lamented the "sure coming of empire" and "the ruin of senatorial prestige."[11] Among the crises of the republic was agrarian reform, which Cicero resisted and which he saw as threatening to the commonwealth. The need for agrarian reform was one of the factors leading to the rising of 1381, the time during which Chaucer was writing The Parliament of Fowls. This work acknowledges agriculture figuratively ("out of olde feldes . . . [c]ometh al this newe corn") but, as David Aers says, pays scant attention to human agency of any kind (22–23).[12] It was not social urgency that renewed the popularity of Cicero's text but dreams. In the fifth century, the text acquired a gloss by Macrobius, The Commentary on the Dream of Scipio, that became the standard medieval guide to the interpretation of dreams and that explains Scipio's place in Chaucer's poems.

Scipio mattered more in Italian literature known to Chaucer than in Chaucer's own writing. Petrarch acknowledged the politics of Cicero's text; Chaucer did not. Petrarch urged at least two figures to assume Scipio's mantle of leadership. In 1364 he called Luchino del Verme the "Veronese Scipio." Earlier, in 1353, Petrarch wrote to Charles IV of Bohemia, making reference to Scipio and, Janet Coleman notes, asking Charles to come to Italy and, "like Caesar," to "revive Rome's political legacy in Cola di Rienzo's place, replacing the ancient republic with a revived imperium Romanum."[13] Charles's daughter, Anne of Bohemia, was Richard's wife. Whether it was Anne or Richard himself who instigated the idea, the king was, two years before his deposition, negotiating with various of his allies to become "king of the Romans" and was even referred to in the Hilary parliament (i.e., January session) of 1397 as "entier Emperour."[14] Hence there was in England, at the end of the fourteenth century, reason for Richard's subjects to be concerned about an "imperium." Chaucer witnessed a struggle between the centralizing monarchy and a decentralizing and representative parliament, but on this potentially dangerous association of Scipio with the imperial ambitions of his monarch Chaucer is—not unexpectedly—silent.

Chaucer, as Rob Pope writes, kept a high personal profile and a low political profile, and thus he enjoyed a stable career at a time when the careers of many others were in deadly turmoil.[15] Chaucer kept his head by producing works that suggest contemporary conditions without becoming imprisoned by them. His sharpest satires against the corrupt clergy in the *Tales*—as illustrated by the Friar, Summoner, and Pardoner—take aim at the lower orders of the clergy, not the bishops in charge of them. Likewise his criticism of court and government is both mild and disguised. This loss of political candor is, in many ways, a net gain for his readers, for the more pointedly a text addresses its own age, the less likely it is to survive it. Exceptions exist—Pope's *The Rape of the Lock*, Dryden's *Mac Flecknoe*—but they require a small digest of contemporary conditions to unlock their social context and their humor.[16]

Chaucer's universalizing power, however, is said to have enabled him to render the human dilemmas of his age as "classical." In her discussion of the place of classical learning in the fourteenth century, Coleman comments that "Chaucer often shows a distinct sense of the past combined with a sense of the eternality of human dilemmas" (Coleman, 49). But the traditional perception of Chaucer as removed from contemporary conflict absolves him of too much responsibility for the historical world in which he was situated as a writer and as an authority. Readers justly credit him with a more encompassing perspective than some of his contemporaries possessed. But Chaucer's genius was not his ability to transcend history. He was a poet of his own age, and to claim that he had a transhistorical perspective suited to our own age is both illogical and misleading. As the example of *The Dream of Scipio* and the events of 1381 show, the timelessness of Chaucer's poetry is created not by a transcendence of history but rather by a double-sided exploitation that amounts to an evasion of it. Chaucer kept his view of contemporary conditions to himself and produced for the public a view that was generalized, moralized, and, to quote Middleton, "pious." This division between public and private frustrates our attempt to understand Chaucer in his context; but the division is both a thematic concern and an operating strategy for *Troilus and Criseyde*. What is an issue for the characters is also an issue for us as readers. The pieties of Chaucer's poetry and its criticism effectively screen social issues; to get to these issues, we must inquire into the division between public and private spheres and look for the "social Chaucer" at the points of their convergence.

2

The Importance of the Work

Readers of medieval texts are often asked about the relevance of the materials they study. Given the mass of contemporary texts inviting explication and analysis, how does one justify the time and energy needed to elaborate on literature in languages so ancient that most people outside the academy must read them in translation?[1] A recent study of Chaucer proposes the unlikely answer that we should read Chaucer for one reason above all others: pleasure.[2] There is no disagreeing that pleasure is a good reason to read Chaucer (or any author). Various pleasures are to be had, but pleasure is not what brings new readers to *Troilus and Criseyde*, although pleasure may bring them back. Instead, as students and teachers, we are usually first summoned to this work by duty. And before duty can lead us to pleasure, we must want to be pleased. Old stories please us when they are linked to our desires and interests; therefore, I propose four points that connect us as modern readers to Chaucer's poem.

First, the story of Troilus and Criseyde has been important to many. *Troilus and Criseyde* impressed its early readers as a legend that captured the much-admired world of antiquity and approximated a classical epic. Chaucer's poem was one in a succession of texts connecting ancient Troy to New Troy, the city of London. Just as the poem reaches backward to an Italian original as well as to Latin and French histories, it also looks forward to adaptations of Chaucer's text, among them Robert Henryson's *The Testament of*

Cresseid, Shakespeare's *Troilus and Cressida,* and a host of lesser-known works, including a translation of part of Chaucer's text into Latin in the seventeenth century. When English readers of the sixteenth and seventeenth centuries were rediscovering and recreating a past for their nation, they included Troy among their chief models, Rome and Athens.

Second, the language of the poem is vital, constituting a turning point in the history of English. For the first time, the resources of the English vernacular were exploited by an author who sought to challenge the towering presence of Latin and the Italian and French vernaculars (a claim that must also be made for the *Tales,* of course). The sources marshaled for *Troilus and Criseyde* include Italian, French, and Latin texts. The wish of Chaucer and his contemporaries that English should be comparable in stature to these languages engaged not only national feeling but also a concern with artistic expression and the capacity of language to preserve the past and reshape it. *Troilus and Criseyde* is distinguished by an exuberant sense of language and its power to mint anew an oft-told tale. The narrator's concern with language increases our intimacy with him: we become aware of tension between the antiquity of the subject and the youthfulness of the language being used to express it.

Third, *Troilus and Criseyde* is both Chaucer's longest narrative and—a surprise to new readers—his most diverse poem. It is a text whose artistic merits have been, almost without exception, lauded by its readers for centuries. All the aspects of Chaucer's art admired in *The Canterbury Tales* are also present in *Troilus and Criseyde.* The reason for the *Tales'* popularity is not their artistic superiority; the story of Troilus was eclipsed partly because of an accident of history and partly because of a hardening of a national tradition in literary taste. Teachers who perpetuate the myth of the *Tales'* superiority do an injustice to Chaucer and to the critical tradition. No student should be encouraged to read the *Tales* because they are more diverse—and therefore more representative—than *Troilus and Criseyde;* the poem's diversity is so great that its readers disagree on the most basic questions raised by the text. Students should instead be encouraged to see the *Tales* and *Troilus* as an interconnected pair.

Fourth, the poem is a challenge, and the reader who comprehends it can command much. *Troilus and Criseyde* is difficult for

11

many reasons, but one too rarely noted is that it forces readers to expect the unexpected. The poem participates in many narrative traditions and intersects with several genres. Its style is mixed and multiple, and that is why the poem has often been compared to a novel and why its psychology has often been praised as modern.[3] It is not a novel, of course, and its psychology is of the poem's age, not our own. But the poem cannot easily be interpreted within a unitary context such as that created by the opening metaphors of springtime that inaugurate the journey to Canterbury. The atmosphere of the *General Prologue* to the *Tales*—the newly-awakened earth, the warm wind and rain, the shoots of new grass, the singing birds—colors the entire work with spiritual optimism and a benevolence that tradition has managed to construe as both Christian and uniquely Chaucerian. Such assumed familiarity, however appealing, naturalizes narrative art and neutralizes social and critical problems that narrative art raises.

The *Canterbury Tales* benefit greatly from Chaucer's use of this naturalizing frame. *Troilus and Criseyde* is also framed, but not with devices of comparable familiarity. Throughout my reading of *Troilus and Criseyde* I employ the frame, an analytical device that produces a familiar opposition between text and context and that operates both in the text and in the history of its reception. Once we see how the poem has been framed by a long history of reading and editing, we will see how many ways there are to understand the poem by looking at and through its narrative, social, sexual, and historical frames.

Two of my four points about the poem's importance stress its context; two emphasize the power of the text and its language. Each of them requires the reader to connect the history of the text, that which is external to the work, to the social world created in and by the text, that which is internal. The opposition between what is internal and external should not be oversimplified or considered permanent and unchanging; the device of the frame will demonstrate how unstable the opposition is. It will become apparent that the four points with which I began this chapter are frames, each attempting to reframe a traditional issue in criticism of *Troilus and Criseyde* as a way of arguing for the work's importance. By reframing my frames, readers undo my work but undertake work of their own and isolate the values they wish to attach to the poem. To frame and reframe is to demystify a work and its critical tradition without degrading the history of either or arguing for or against the work's status as a "classic." The study of the frame is a way to read texts and to learn about one's own habits and desires as a reader. Such learning is not only one of the great rewards but also one of the greatest pleasures that literary texts offer.

3

Critical Reception
and the History of the Work

The reader new to *Troilus and Criseyde* might expect a discussion of the work's critical reception to survey the modern critical tradition, divided into approaches according to their historical succession. In my view, the order of history is important, the survey of criticism less so. The major critical issues of the poem have been summarized by Alice Kaminsky; recent bibliographies are rich in other assessments.[1] My aim is not to categorize modern literary criticism but to recover major ideas in the history of readings of *Troilus and Criseyde*.

EARLY EDITORIAL HISTORY

The editorial tradition of *Troilus and Criseyde* is part of a larger hermeneutic, interpretive tradition. Because all editing is a way of reading, the poem's critical reception begins with its manuscripts and with the interpretations of its first readers. The poem is found in 16 manuscripts, the earliest from the early fifteenth century, and a small number of fragments. In addition, three early printed editions present texts independent of the manuscripts (although one of these editions is independent for only a few hundred lines of the first book).[2] Caroline F. E. Spurgeon, who has constructed a six-

14

part survey of allusions to Chaucer's work from 1357 to 1900,[3] characterizes the century after Chaucer's death, the first period of critical reception, as rich in "enthusiastic and reverential praise" from the poet's contemporaries and successors (Spurgeon, x). But these readers were aware that *Troilus and Criseyde* was a peculiar poem, and those who copied the text acted on their responses to it. As a result, the manuscripts differ considerably, ranging from different readings of individual lines to omission of certain parts of the text.

The readings and misreadings of early scribes can be studied in Barry A. Windeatt's superb edition, which includes readings from various manuscripts and which also prints the poem's chief source, Boccaccio's *Il Filostrato*.[4] As scribes copied *Troilus and Criseyde*, they sometimes deleted parts of it. Three sections—the song of Troilus in book 3 (3.1744-71), his long speech about free will in book 4 (4.958-1082), and his ascent through the spheres in book 5 (5.1807-27)—were omitted several times, creating the suspicion that the lines were either later additions or material about which Chaucer had second thoughts (Windeatt, *TC*, 38-40). Less drastic than omission is the scribes' tendency to rewrite some expressions into more ornate speech, "as if the simplicity of Chaucer's diction [were] inadequate to the scribe's sense of the context" (Windeatt, *TC*, 28-29). In book 2, Pandarus advises Troilus on how to write a letter to Criseyde: "I woot thow nylt it dygneliche endite" (2.1024; "I know you won't write in a haughty fashion"). "Dygneliche" was, in various manuscripts, changed to "papally," "clergaly" (ingeniously), "clerkissly" (learnedly), and "digneliche ny mysteliche" (proudly nor abstractly). Windeatt observes that the scribes, in changing this line about scribal activity (about writing), were responding to what they found "distinctive in the poem's diction and syntax" (Windeatt, *TC*, 27). Sometimes the scribes removed striking features, for example, altering the image of an eagle's feathers as "whit as bone" to "whit as milk" (2.926). It seems as if the scribes sought to participate in the creation of the poem, responding sympathetically to the characters and changing emphasis by substituting their own words for Chaucer's. Such changes are not errors, although they are easily seen as such; they blur the line between what is "in the text" and what is not, between those who read and those who write, a distinction modern readers too find problematic.

In the second period Spurgeon describes (late fifteenth and early sixteenth centuries), editors joined scribes in fixing and reshaping Chaucer's reputation by enlarging the canon of works attributed to him. The first printed edition of *Troilus and Criseyde* was produced by William Caxton in 1483, the year in which he published the second edition of *The Canterbury Tales* and an edition of *The House of Fame*. Caxton printed a transcript of a single manuscript rather than a "critical" edition, which is compiled from several manuscripts and which joins different strands of the textual tradition. Caxton's edition was reprinted in 1517 by Wynkyn de Worde and again in 1526 by Richard Pynson. Pynson added several amatory poems (none authentic) to the canon.[5]

These misattributed works did not escape suspicion for long. William Thynne, the next editor of *Troilus and Criseyde*, knew that some works credited to Chaucer were not authentic.[6] Robert K. Root writes that Thynne's text, published in 1532, is "easily the best edition of the poem published before the nineteenth century," for it "is really edited, being based on a collation of several authorities."[7] Thynne removed some of Pynson's additions but contributed his own. His chief addition was to print—as an appendix (in effect, a sixth book) to *Troilus and Criseyde—The Testament of Cresseid* by Robert Henryson, a work falsely ascribed to Chaucer that traveled with his poem for many years.[8] Thynne also attached *The Plowman's Tale* to his 1542 edition,[9] a text that helped Chaucer acquire a reputation (unlikely as it seems to us) as a social reformer and critic of religious abuses. Although Chaucer's satires of corrupt clergy are among the most powerful stories found in *The Canterbury Tales*, his orthodoxy in matters ecclesiastical is rarely doubted. It was only because of *The Plowman's Tale*—and, later, *Jack Upland*—that he was seen as a reformer. These texts expressed antipapal and anticlerical sentiments that were advocated by Henry VIII and his court in order to break with Rome and to establish the Church of England.

In 1561 John Stow reprinted Thynne's edition. Stow's edition, considered derivative of, and in some ways inferior to, Thynne's, was probably the major text of Chaucer available to both Spenser and Shakespeare.[10] Stow renewed Thynne's influence and promoted Chaucer's emergence as a major figure in the new category of "national" or "English" authors whose prestige could be used to

16

further political causes. Henry's court has been called "an unofficial center for Chaucer studies" during the 1520s and 1530s.[11] By the middle of the century, when Elizabeth I had succeeded to the throne, curiosity about the origins and nature of the English language stimulated the recovery of the linguistic heritage of Anglo-Saxon England (c. A.D. 600–1100), whose language and culture were already ancient in Chaucer's time.

Stow was one of a number of scholars at work with manuscripts of both Old and Middle English. He was acquainted with the circle of Matthew Parker, the archbishop of Canterbury who, at Elizabeth's request, published *A Testimonie of Antiquitie* in 1565–66, a book long regarded as the first modern edition of Anglo-Saxon texts. John Bale and John Leland, two early scholars at work on the national literary tradition, sought to rescue ancient books from the destruction of monastic libraries that followed the dissolution of monasteries under Henry VIII. Both included biographies of Chaucer in their literary histories of England (both in Latin), the first such accounts to be written, to which they appended lists of Chaucer's works (derived from Thynne's 1526 edition). Another scholarly polemicist was John Foxe, whose *Ecclesiasticall History* of 1570 listed Chaucer among the "faithful witnesses" who protested the corruption of the clergy in the fourteenth century.[12] Foxe's text of *Jack Upland* was used by a later editor, Thomas Speght, who saw affinities between this text and *The Plowman's Tale* as securing claims of Chaucer's authorship of both.[13] Foxe marveled that the Catholic bishops, who had destroyed so many dangerous books that "might bryng the people to any light of knowledge," would have allowed Chaucer's to be printed. Foxe's conclusion was that Chaucer, by convincing the bishops that the works were mere jests, had concealed his controversial views of religion and the church "vnder shadows couertly, as vnder a visoure he suborneth truth."[14]

Up to this point, the tradition of Chaucer scholarship readily identifies him with contemporary social causes. In the third period defined by Spurgeon, the sixteenth century, Chaucer was first viewed with something like a critical attitude, and two new features appear in the tradition. In 1598 Speght published the first of two editions of Chaucer's works containing a biography of the poet and a glossary explicating "hard words," intended not only to help readers understand Chaucer but also to improve their own vocabularies. Part of a developing sense of scholarly method, these features also mark a new awareness of Chaucer's writing as unfamiliar. They are signs that Chaucer's language and personality had begun to dim; the poet could be seen as a great "English" author only with scholarly assistance.

Speght's edition was reissued in 1602 with many additions and corrections developed with the assistance of Francis Thynne, William Thynne's son. In the first edition (1598) Speght did not consult manuscripts, but in the second, issued just four years later, with Thynne's help, he did so and went on to take credit for some improvements to Stow's 1561 edition. In both the first and the second editions, Speght augmented the text with explanatory notes and added works to Chaucer's canon (*The Flower and the Leaf, The Isle of Ladies*) that retained their place until the nineteenth century.[15] There are signs that a more accurate knowledge of Chaucer's style and work was taking shape. For example, Thynne showed, in 1599, that *The Testament of Cresseid* was not Chaucer's. Nonetheless, the poem appears in Speght's edition and continued to be attributed to Chaucer for many years. Speght's second edition added new materials to Chaucer's canon, including the anticlerical *Jack Upland.*[16]

Speght's *Troilus* was reprinted in 1687, nearly a century after the second edition. That this text remained the standard for nearly a century and that Chaucer's most famous readers—including Milton, Dryden, and Pope—knew Chaucer from this edition testify to the durability of Speght's edition. But the lack of new editions also indicates that the seventeenth century, the fourth period, was a low point in Chaucer's reputation. Readers regarded *Troilus and Criseyde* as a masterful demonstration of rhetorical style. But increasingly in this period readers regarded the poet's language as rough, even barbaric and unreadable, and considered his meter defective. Speght realized that Chaucer's meter was not as irregular as other readers thought, but few shared Speght's view of Chaucer's "numbers."[17] Chaucer continued to be hailed as a great writer, but his works had had their day. "By the end of the century," Spurgeon writes, "Chaucer was frankly looked upon as antiquated and barbaric by the highest authorities in these matters" (Spurgeon, 1:xxx). She quotes Joseph Addison's view from *An Ac-*

count *of the Greatest English Poets* (1694) as a typical view of Chaucer:

> But Age has Rusted what the Poet writ,
> Worn out his Language and obscur'd his Wit:
> In vain he jests in his unpolish'd strain
> And tries to make his Readers laugh in vain.

Spurgeon charitably notes that Addison was only 21 when he expressed this view (Spurgeon, 1:xxx; quotation from Addison, 266).

The fourth period was concluded and Spurgeon's fifth period begun by Dryden's *Preface to Fables Ancient and Modern* (1700), which included translations of some of *The Canterbury Tales*. Dryden admired Chaucer's achievement but expressed tolerant, indeed patronizing, reservations about the deficiencies in his art. Nonetheless, Dryden celebrated Chaucer as a representative of English national character: "He must have been a man of a most wonderful comprehensive nature, because, as it has been truly observed of him, he has taken into the compass of his *Canterbury Tales* the various manners and humors (as we now call them) of the whole English nation in his age. Not a single character has escaped him. All his pilgrims are severally distinguished from each other; and not only in their inclinations but in their very physiognomies and persons." He concludes, "'Tis sufficient to say, according to the proverb, that here is God's plenty."[18] With this comment, designed to assure his readers that Chaucer's age was no different from their own, Dryden drew attention to the author as a voice of national artistic and moral excellence. He thereby inaugurated a new period in Chaucer criticism. Chaucer's status never declined after this point, although *Troilus and Criseyde* began to lose place to *The Canterbury Tales* as the poet's most favored creation.

Spurgeon notes that in the third and fourth of her six periods of Chaucerian reception *Troilus and Criseyde* was dominant. There are some 117 references to the poem up to 1700, compared to only 53 to the *Tales* as a whole. Following Dryden's modernization, the numbers begin to shift. Up to 1750, there were 124 additional references to *Troilus* and 59 to the *Tales*. But in the next fifty years, Spurgeon finds 19 references to the *Tales* but only 5 to *Troilus*, and in the next century she finds 24 for the *Tales* and 13 for *Troilus*. Of course individual tales were also frequently mentioned, in particular the tales by the Knight, the Nun's Priest, and the Wife of Bath (Spurgeon, 1:lxxix).

The change was not due to Dryden alone, of course, but rather to the developing consciousness of English national literature, the awakenings of which we have seen already in the sixteenth century. But with Dryden and others the idea of the great Englishman as great English author, and poet in particular, acquires special importance. In such a climate it is easy to see why the "natural" speech of *The Canterbury Tales* would replace the artifice of *Troilus and Criseyde*. *Troilus and Criseyde* resembles an epic. So long as classical forms were more important than English imitations of them, and so long as the recovery of classical culture dominated literary life in England, *Troilus* would be England's most obvious link to the medieval past. But when the ideal shifted to exposition of national character, the *Tales* overtook the courtly romance as representative of "God's plenty."

Yet the editorial tradition of *Troilus and Criseyde* continued. A new collation of manuscripts was undertaken by John Urry for his edition of 1721. Urry's work was extremely inconsistent, and Root denounces his edition as "the high-water mark of corruption."[19] The edition was actually a collaborative project involving nine other scholars and was concluded only after Urry's death. But even this edition is not without merit. For example, the editors made successful attempts (but not, as we see with Speght's work, the first attempts) to remove certain works from the canon, such as Henryson's *The Testament of Cresseid*, which had been mistakenly attributed to Chaucer for so long.[20] And Urry's edition, however defective, includes illustrations of various Canterbury pilgrims and—all the better—of the editor and Chaucer, both particularly handsome.[21] It is much to be regretted that the great eighteenth-century editor Thomas Tyrwhitt did not edit *Troilus and Criseyde* along with his four-volume edition of *The Canterbury Tales*, which appeared in 1775 (with a glossary in 1778), a work considered to be the first competent edition of the text. Windeatt calls Tyrwhitt "the founder of modern Chaucer editing" and applauds not only his understanding of Chaucer's language but his commentary on the texts, drawn from his vast knowledge of continental literature, Chaucer's sources, and medieval views of the world.[22] *Troilus and*

Criseyde was not reedited from manuscripts after Urry until Robert Bell's edition of 1854–56. Intervening editions—those by John Bell (1782), Robert Anderson (1793–95), Alexander Chalmers (1810), and others—reprinted editions before Urry's.[23]

What Chaucer acquired through Dryden in Spurgeon's fifth period he acquired from the academy in the period inaugurated by Tyrwhitt, Spurgeon's sixth phase. Scholarly editions became frequent in the nineteenth century. Richard Morris reedited all of Chaucer in 1866, and in 1894 Walter Skeat's *Oxford Chaucer* appeared, followed in 1898 by the Globe Edition of Chaucer's complete works. The next edition was Root's own, of 1926.[24] Of recent editions of *Troilus and Criseyde* the reader has many to choose. *The Riverside Chaucer*, a revision of F. N. Robinson's second edition of 1953, is the modern standard. New editions are in progress, chief among them the ambitious project of the New Chaucer Society to produce "variorum" texts of all of Chaucer's works.[25]

READERS' RESPONSES

A survey of the history of reading *Troilus and Criseyde* shows us how early some issues in the modern tradition were identified. The first to take up the story after Chaucer was John Lydgate, whose massive *Troy Book* was begun in 1420 at the request of Henry V, who also owned a luxurious manuscript of *Troilus and Criseyde*.[26] Lydgate's work became the standard late medieval and Renaissance source on the city and its history and was known to Shakespeare and many others.[27] The outstanding feature of this tradition is not the decline of Troy, however, but the degradation of Criseyde. The most important elaboration of Criseyde's fate is Henryson's *The Testament of Cresseid.* Henryson is the chief figure of the "Scottish Chaucerians," a group of authors who imitated the poet's verse forms (in particular *rime royale*) and borrowed his subjects and genres, including the dream vision.[28] Henryson's authorship was unrecognized long after this work appeared and Chaucer was credited with it (Henryson's dates are still unknown [c. 1440?–1505?]). Henryson's poem begins where Chaucer's story concludes, with Troilus's death and Criseyde's uncertain future among the Greeks.

21

Henryson describes how she contracted leprosy as punishment for her sexual excesses and eventually was forgiven for betraying her lover. His poem is regarded as "the most artistic, the most powerful handling [of the subject] made by any poet after Chaucer."[29] Henryson was not the first to speculate on her reputation, however. In *Philip Sparrow* (1507) John Skelton scoffed at the hero and criticized Criseyde, whose name had already been tarnished in popular ballads.[30] But in 1523 Skelton used Criseyde to compliment Lady Elizabeth Howard, exalting her as a "model mistress" (Rollins, 390).

The development of the legend of Criseyde's degradation, curiously, is heavily indebted to Chaucer, since Henryson's version of her history as a leper was attributed to Chaucer. Even though the playwrights who took up the case against her saw themselves as continuing Chaucer's narrative, Chaucer's narrator's attitude toward her is ambivalent and certainly not openly condemnatory. In 1562 Arthur Brooke published the *Tragicall Historye of Romeus and Iuliet*, translated from an Italian play by Bandell; the *Tragicall Historye* both quotes Chaucer's poem and imitates it. Brooke's work was one of the chief sources for Shakespeare's *Romeo and Juliet* (Spurgeon, 3:29–33). More directly related to Chaucer's work, of course, is Shakespeare's *Troilus and Cressida*, a work that Rollins credits with pulling Criseyde "out of the mire in which Henryson's followers had placed her." Many plays and poems denounced Criseyde, as Rollins and Spurgeon show (Rollins, 429; Spurgeon, 3:42–43), a tradition that did not end, apparently, until Dryden intervened. In his dramatic version of the story, *Troilus and Cresside, or Truth Found Too Late* (1679), he invented the myth of Criseyde's constancy.

Tudor admiration for Chaucer found expression in two forms: rhetorical analysis and drama. While Foxe praised Chaucer's skill at concealing theological convictions "under a visoure," poets concerned chiefly with courtly guises had already (by 1555) made Chaucer's verse a fashion. In the sixteenth century, in the court of Henry VII, *Troilus and Criseyde* was admired not only as an example of English love poetry but as an example of highly ornate art valued far above the "common speech" of *The Canterbury Tales*. Given Chaucer's knowledge of Petrarch and given the status of the Italian sonnet in the Renaissance, it is easy to understand why Chaucer's poetry was prized as an early attempt to achieve the cultural borrowing accomplished by the humanists only two hundred years after his death. *Troilus and Criseyde* furnished court poets, including Sir Thomas Wyatt, with both inspiration, and models of diction.[31]

The influence of *Troilus and Criseyde* on rhetoric emerges most clearly in George Puttenham's *Arte of English Poesie* (1589). Puttenham's work is one of the great "defenses" of poetry written in English (after Italian precedents) to explain why vernacular verse was not a threat to Christian piety. Puttenham uses *Troilus and Criseyde* to illustrate no fewer than 25 literary devices, showing how fully the poem's elaborate artifice was understood. Puttenham ranked Chaucer (especially as author of *Troilus and Criseyde*) above Gower, Lydgate, and Langland, but he also asserted that these authors should no longer be imitated, for "their language is out of vse with vs."[32]

Not all readings of the poem were amorous, however. *Disce Mori*, a mid-fifteenth-century treatise for women religious that discusses carnal and spiritual love, quotes the first part of the first "Song" of Troilus ("If no love is, O God, what fele I so?" [1.400–420]). *Troilus and Criseyde* was valued from the first as a great story about two kinds of love, friendship and sexual passion. The difference between *amicitia* (friendship) and *amor* (sexual love) was used to illustrate a list of seven ways of distinguishing these two kinds of love from each other. At first a treatise seems to be a curious place to find a quotation from a love poem, but, as Lee Patterson has shown, one of this poem's major ethical ideas is the tension between sexual love and the love that comes as part of genuine friendship.[33]

In addition to ballads, plays, and this treatise, rewritings of Chaucer's poem included translation into Latin and modern English. The strangest reworking is a translation of the first two books of the poem into Latin, *Amorum Troili et Creseidae libri duo priores Anglico-Latini*, published by Sir Francis Kinaston in 1635. Kinaston, who based his work on Speght's, added several prefatory poems to his translation, many of them lamenting that Chaucer had "died" in his decayed English and vowing that he would live again. The verse by Francis James commends Kinaston for making a pilgrimage to Rome "and sothly there lerne Latine verse," juxtaposing the center of classical culture with Canterbury, the pilgrimage center of English Christianity (Spurgeon, 1:212–13). Its place here, however, is its commentary on the state of Chaucer's English: better, that is, to preserve the text in Latin than allow it to decay further in a language too few could read.

Virtually contemporary with the translation is a "modernization" of the poem published by Jonathan Sidnam in 1630, *A Paraphrase upon the Three First Books of Chaucer's Troilus and Cressida Translated into Our Moderne English.* Sidnam's work was not published until 1960 and survived up to that time in a single manuscript. As Herbert G. Wright points out, a modernization must modify a medieval setting and reconceptualize cultural and historical variables. Sidnam changed Chaucer's references to the pagan gods and emphasized the poem's Christian theology. (*Troilus and Criseyde* itself mixes these systems; early scribes also Christianized pagan references.) Physical space is another example. Many have commented on the importance of privacy in the poem and the difficulty of obtaining it when women of Criseyde's status were surrounded by attendants and were rarely completely alone. In book 2, when Pandarus and Criseyde are speaking of Troilus, Pandarus indicates the delicacy of the subject and pretends to leave her company. She detains him, and her attendants "that herde that," taking the clue, "gan fer awey to stonde" (2.216). Sidnam's version indicates that the attendants not only stand back but "quitt the roome, and left it to them free / That soe they might discourse more priuatelie." Sidnam was also conscious that Chaucer's audience is constantly summoned to *listen* in the original. At the start of book 2, for example, the narrator asks if there is any lover that "herkneth"—that is, that listens (2:29–31). Sidnam's audience read as well as listened: he writes to "anie louer neere this place / W[hi]ch redes this storie, or shall heare men saie."34 Sidnam's audience was also quite particular about what they heard. Sidnam stopped with book 3 because after that point Criseyde's behavior was too despicable to describe. Completely lacking in sympathy for her, he chose to terminate the translation rather than to tell the story of her infidelity. Such moralized readings of Chaucer's poem may strike us as more "medieval" than the poem itself. But such a conclusion is contradictory, for the sexual ambiguity Chaucer wrote into *Troilus and Criseyde* was inescapably medieval. It is the postmedieval narrowing of the text that we should note, for we then see successive hands—scribes', editors', translators'—striving to frame and restrict Chaucer's meaning, eliminating ambiguity and emphasizing a Christian perspective.

My survey seeks to draw the reader new to Chaucer to the early reception of *Troilus and Criseyde* and to incorporate the history of the discipline into the study of the poem. Although the history of Chaucer scholarship seems to be derivative and secondary to Chaucer's texts—it appears to be intellectual history rather than literary criticism—there are many fronts on which the incorporation of this history into criticism is vital. I will give only two. The first is that all of Chaucer's editors were his readers and interpreters, responding to the politics and aesthetics of his text in ways similar to our own. In the Reformation his readers attributed Protestant morality to Chaucer's poetry. As late as 1870 James Russell Lowell commended the poet as "a reformer, too, not only in literature, but in morals."[35] In the midtwentieth century, historical critics sought to align Chaucer with an equally exclusive (and equally anachronistic) moral outlook derived from Saint Augustine and other scriptural exegetes.[36] Renaissance dramatists delighted in degrading Criseyde as a paradigm of fallen womanhood; she has had her critics in the modern age, but today she is usually defended, often with a passion as righteous as that of her early detractors.

The second reason to consider the history of the discipline is that critical self-consciousness, an important goal of reading, depends on a consciousness of history. History surrounds Chaucer's poetry as plainly in the centuries after the poet's death as it did during his lifetime. Whether we are interested in the history of poetic styles, history of the language, political history, or social history, we can see at every point in the reception of *Troilus and Criseyde* that Chaucer's work was "social" in its readers' eyes: it spoke to readers about their own interests. Our interest in the poem is, therefore, a way to develop an interest in the history we share with all its readers, a history that designated literary periods ("medieval" and "Renaissance" in particular) urge us to fragment.[37] By seeing the poem as "social" in this sense we lessen the sense of isolation from contemporary life that Chaucer imposed on his text. Simultaneously, we lessen our sense of isolation from medieval and early modern cultures, and that is surely all to the good.

A Reading

¶

4

Looking through and at the Frame

THE TEXT AND THE SUBJECT

Troilus and Criseyde was once admired as Chaucer's finest poem, and many readers still consider it his masterpiece. But no matter how highly we estimate its merits, we cannot underestimate its difficulties. Certain features that readers find so engaging in *The Canterbury Tales*—the vivacious narrator, variety in tone and language, and mix of humor and high seriousness—are also found in *Troilus*. But Chaucer's "litel bok," as he called *Troilus and Criseyde*, is dense and difficult. Its mighty subject is constrained within a small compass, and the resulting compression both enhances the reader's experience and complicates it.

Troilus and Criseyde contains 8,239 lines, nearly half the length of the poetic *Tales*. To describe a poem so large as having a small compass may seem ill-advised; there is no mistaking that *Troilus and Criseyde* is not a "litel bok" but a big one. Yet everything about it, from stanzaic form to narrative structure, is carefully shaped and minutely calculated. The verse is written in *rime royale*, a stanza with seven lines and three rhymes; it is an exacting measure used to create both intimate dialogue and sweeping narration, with a form precise and delicate, yet also powerful. Much in the poem is equally stylized; if not static, the work is characterized by insistent repetition. There are numerous parallel scenes (at windows, in gardens, in bedrooms), and key images and thoughts are represented by many characters, including the narrator. The poem is divided into five books, each divided into two parts, with a prologue or (in the case of the last book) an epilogue serving as commentary on the rest of the book. Simply as a tale told in a demanding verse form, with a structure finely articulated yet fluid, *Troilus and Criseyde* is a virtuoso performance.

Form is one source of the poem's power. Another—unexpectedly—is its undisguised pessimism. *Troilus and Criseyde* does not offer a vision of Chaucer's society, which, after Dryden, so many have wanted to find in the *Tales*, but rather a vision of an ancient world in which a conventional love story plays itself out unhappily during a ruinous war. The buoyant optimism that characterizes the Canterbury pilgrimage, evoked by the world in springtime and its promise of regeneration, is, in a poetic gesture of considerable risk, banished at the outset of *Troilus*. Readers of the *Tales* greatly enjoy the sense of the fitness of things that Chaucer achieves as the pilgrims, having competed with and corrected each other, finally fall silent behind the Parson's edifying discourse. This is a "solempne servise," to borrow words from *The Book of the Duchess* (302), fit to conclude a great pilgrimage. Few have questioned Chaucer's decision to end a narrative of seeming tolerance for sin with a sermon about penance; it is a touch (even if not entirely original) that the ages could envy.

In *Troilus and Criseyde*, however, the reader is unsettled from the start by a sense of the unfitness of things. In a world at war, the poem opens with a father's betrayal of both his country, Troy, and his daughter, Criseyde. With their awareness of war heightened by Calkas's desertion, the citizens first shun but then draw around her. At a festival inside this renewed peace and order, Troilus and Criseyde meet; soon they are lovers. As the war drags on, the communal bond that protects Criseyde is tested; public promises are broken and private betrayals follow. The destruction of Troy, imposed from outside but invited by internal weakness, nears. But *Troilus and Criseyde* does not conclude with military disaster. Instead, Chaucer's "palinode" sweeps war to one side, sexual love to another, and closes with an ornate prayer.

Rather than try to interpret this complex and contradictory text within a single thematic focus, I propose to analyze the poem as a text that represents its subjects both in terms of the roles created for them by communal and political structures and in terms of their private, interior selves. As I emphasized in the first chapter, the social conflicts of the poem are not the particular conflicts of Chaucer's world. But *Troilus and Criseyde* is "social" nonetheless, for it operates within a nexus of institutional loyalties involving individuals, the family, the king, and the parliament within Troy, and, indirectly, involving the individuals and institutions of Chaucer's London. *Troilus and Criseyde* takes place in antiquity, rather than in Chaucer's "here and now" (which is still ancient to us), making it difficult to reconfigure the social systems of Troy as fourteenth-century institutions, much less as the institutions of our own time. In order to establish these connections between Chaucer's poem and its contexts, we need to recognize *Troilus and Criseyde* as a poem about human behavior under multiple stresses: a love affair, a war, a compelling need for secrecy, an unwritten but powerful code that governs both intimate and public behavior and thus organizes the poem's social worlds. The tensions of the poem extend to and echo within the social worlds of the poem's medieval and modern readers.

But more than analogies between the medieval and the modern are necessary if we are to understand the social energies of Chaucer's poem. We need to think of literary characters and their behavior in something other than the categories traditionally pro- posed for them. Students often are warned against approaching characters as "real people," just as they are warned about reading texts to find the "hidden meaning" or concealed symbolic content. But certain ideas about characters as "natural" or "realistic" persist and need to be examined more closely. When C. David Benson writes that "*Troilus and Criseyde* is a story about human beings," he means that it is about people rather than animals or allegorical figures. His claims that the poem is about "fully developed, natu- ralistic men and women," however, steer the reader too far toward assumptions about character that are problematic even for modern, not to mention for medieval, texts.[1] The point that literary charac- ters are not, in fact, "naturalistic" men and women, cannot be made too often. Readers traditionally understand character as either realistic (mimetic) or allegorical (and therefore transhistorical). Some argue that the poet created characters who speak autobio- graphically, in a dramatic and confessional mode; others stress the role of allegorical types—for example, traditional vice figures—in his portrayal of character.[2]

But our choices are not confined to these two models. Underlying either model is another idea of character as shaped by language and social relations, two interconnected forces that help to constitute the identities of those persons whom the relations engage and connect. The characters in Chaucer's poem are not personalities who exist outside the language of the text; rather, they are created by it. As we respond to Troilus and Criseyde as realistically drawn characters (which they are), we must also see them as what contemporary criticism calls "subjects." Lee Patterson claims that, in the modern world, we tend to believe that "human life is conceived in terms of a basic unit, the autonomous, free, self-determining individual" possessed of an independent will and able to choose freely. Against this idea, the combined forces of social criticism and linguistic analysis assert the importance of two determining factors: first, social structures that sharply limit the choices an individual can make; second, language itself, which limits the speaking positions available to us and constitutes the very selfhood that we thought language expressed.[3]

The importance of subjectivity to literary character can be exaggerated. Patterson seems to suggest that academics have somehow taken the lead in identifying the limits to the individual autonomy that quite ordinary people recognize as the inevitable consequences of living within traditional social structures (Patterson, 5). But such extremes should be avoided, for the idea of the subject opens many doors to readers of Chaucer. Writing of the narrative voices of *The Canterbury Tales*, H. Marshall Leicester, Jr., observes that the tales "concentrate not on the way preexisting persons create language but on the way language creates people." In modern critical theory, he writes, "the subject is not conceived as a substantial thing, like a rock, but as a position in a larger structure, a site through which various forces pass."[4] Criseyde, Troilus, and Pandarus do not exist outside Chaucer's text; within it they are not individuals who exist independent of their society or who float within it at liberty to choose their situations and conditions. They can be compared to other Chaucerian characters who find "what they can use in their own traditions and culture" to express themselves and solve their problems, thus demonstrating, Leicester writes, "how personality itself—the subject—is institutionally con-structed, not as an unconscious *expression* of institutional struc-ture and power, but as the result of the active *use* of them."[5] To say that these characters are "sites" through which the power and his-tory of Trojan society flows, is—temporarily—to de-humanize the characters by redefining their status in terms of hierarchies of power and influence. Their identities are constituted by their lan-guage and by the social roles available to them, not only by individ-ual consciousness, which is the traditional site of personality and of literary character.[6]

The linguistic and the social inevitably merge, for the social conventions of Troy are created through the literary language of Chaucer's London and its conventions. Chaucer's choice of Troy, the Trojan war, and the Trojan court as his subjects, and even his choice of the English language as his medium, to which he calls attention in his conclusion (5.1793–99), are social acts. Through these choices the conventions of Troy register the conventions of Chaucer's London. Chaucer took his models from other literary works and also, we can safely presume, from life. But he did not create characters that others in his time could not have imagined; Chaucer's characters are deeply conventional. To see them as "subjects" is to define their conventionality both in terms of their social positions within Troy and in terms of the linguistic and liter-ary repertory from which Chaucer drew.

Against the impersonal concept of the character as the subject, which emphasizes a lack of freedom, it is useful to assert the tradi-tional idea of the character as an individual who is free and psycho-logically complex. In *Troilus and Criseyde* each character expresses his or her views both in public and in the realm of private, interior reality. One important measure of the characters' complexity is the balance that they seek to maintain between exterior and interior forces. The characters know that their speech—their public dis-course—must be closely guarded and their secrets kept. Their inte-rior selves respond to the social possibilities available to them—that is, ideas of who they are, and how they should act and speak, that are Chaucerian ideas of the ideal transferred onto them.

The dichotomy between the private and the public operates throughout *Troilus and Criseyde*. Public codes dictate social roles and help to constitute the characters who must function within them. But at the same time the characters possess private, interior spaces in which their secrets and unspoken thoughts and desires reside. Their private identities allow them to move among various social groups but force them to shield their private desires from public scrutiny. Indeed, the whole of *Troilus and Criseyde* is shaped by a powerful need for secrecy. This need cannot be entirely rationalized, as it usually is, as the demand of the code of "courtly love." For this code was not, and is not in the poem, a self-contained entity or a mere abstraction, a set of rules for the entertainment of the aristocracy. It is instead a social system that dispenses and disperses power according to the requirements of an acknowledged hierarchy. The demand for silence entailed by the code is also a demand for compliance with traditional structures that frame the poem.

The need for silence requires that the characters behave in certain ways. Other forces exert similar pressures. To help readers identify and analyze these forces and gauge their impact on the poem's subjects, I look at *Troilus and Criseyde* through the frame. A metaphor for the work of criticism and appreciation, the frame performs both internal and external functions, dividing the aesthetics of art, or its inside, from the nonaesthetic world outside art. Frames also divide the text's social and symbolic systems and help us detect the forces at work inside Chaucer's text.

THE FRAME

The frame is explicitly theoretical without being unfamiliar (as many theoretical apparatuses are). We know frames as picture frames, but there are many kinds of frames: the screens of movie theaters, stages, the pages of a book that surround text with white space, television sets, and computer monitors. As John Frow writes in *Marxism and Literary History*, numerous frames surround acts of reading and writing, making statements and demands as they establish the limits to our vision.[7] Scholarly editions, popular (less detailed) student or "teaching" editions, and translations are also frames, and around them we readily see the framing force of large publishing houses and the corporate conglomerates that enclose

34

them. But all frames are not equal. Some editions carry greater authority than others. And all frames are not apparent. Translations, for example, serve as interpretations and may suppress elements (for example, the sexually explicit) that professional readers consider too dangerous for students.[8]

We ordinarily think of the frame as marginal and the picture as central, a distinction that parallels a traditional division between form and content, between aesthetic text and nonaesthetic context. But it is difficult to divide the frame from the work of art. Even a picture without a frame is "framed" by the line that divides it from the wall it hangs on, for that edge isolates the work of art from its context. The frame is not simply a passive support; instead, it defines space and controls assertions about art displayed within it. Frow observes that a toilet seat, when it is moved from a bathroom to a museum wall, becomes a work of art. "The toilet seat hung in a museum is an aesthetic object because the museum sanctions its situation as aesthetic," Frow writes (220). That is, the museum wall *frames* the toilet seat and transforms its significance. To help us understand the literary implications of the frame, I will illustrate three kinds of framing activity.

One commonly understood kind of frame, the unifying framework of narrative, was a traditional literary device already in Chaucer's time. The concept of literary framework figures prominently in criticism of *The Canterbury Tales*, which is a collection held together—framed—by the metaphor of pilgrimage.[9] This unifying frame is frequently used to link tellers to tales and thereby to establish causality and intentionality as means of interpreting the *Tales*. This is a mechanical, if reliable, device that is used to demonstrate correspondences between the personalities of the pilgrims and the style and content of their narratives. Tale-teller relationships are particularly effective frames, but they rarely invite students to examine the claims about psychological realism on which those relationships are based.

A second kind of frame is genre, which is the most familiar of the various frames operating within the *Tales*. Frow defines the frame as "a metaphor for the frame structures of genre and literary system" (220). I will discuss the operations of genre and literary system separately. Genre both leads us into the text and restricts our access to it. When we are told that "The Miller's Tale" is a fabliau, the fabliau genre begins to condition our interpretation of the text. When we learn that *Troilus and Criseyde* is traditionally understood as a tragedy, the poem *becomes* a tragedy: the frame of genre adheres to the identity of the work, and readers see the text as "the tragedy of *Troilus and Criseyde*." But the poem is also understood as a romance, a genre that frames the text with different expectations. Depending on the frame one imposes, the poem is romance or tragedy or even a "Boethian" comedy, a philosophical work about moral growth through good acts.[10] Filled with letters, songs, and dreams, each set off as a separate creation, the poem also participates in many moods, sometimes heavy with foreboding, sometimes fully in the spirit of "The General Prologue" to the *Tales*. Each change, each swing from tragic lament to high comedy, evokes the presence of a new literary frame, creates closure, and urges certain interpretive conclusions upon us.

My third division is the category of literary system. Frow uses the term "literary system" to indicate the operations of frames outside the artist's control as well as the artist's work itself. Frames outside the author's control include reputation, critical reception, editorial handling, and translation, factors which, as we have already seen in chapter 3, can influence reading as forcefully as the author's own resources. Chaucer's standing as the greatest fourteenth-century English poet has conditioned both editorial traditions and interpretations of his works as "typical" examples of medieval forms. The anthology is an institutional frame, a "literary system" that augments the power of authorial identity and editorial practice. Those *Tales* included in the *Norton Anthology*, for example, are considered representative of Chaucer and perhaps even regarded as the best of his works.

The framing functions of "literary system" that matter most to my analysis are those that operate within texts. Frow comments that the frame differentiates the "real" from "symbolic" and defines the text's "appropriate degrees of fictionality and figurality and the kinds of use to which it can be put" (Frow, 220). Frames that operate within texts identify what I call "symbolic structures," which are images, behavioral codes, and other patterns of organization within larger social structures that govern the world of the poem. Within texts, frames separate social context from symbolic content. They stand between symbolic structures, which present the ideals of the social order, and the social order that is governed by and that perpetuates these structures. This division between symbolic and social orders, comparable to that between the ideal and the real, distinguishes the way things are (the social) from the way tradition and communities of authors and authorities say they should be (the symbolic).

Symbolic structures attach value to persons, sexes, events, words, actions, and to those modes of existence and communication that combine to organize social relations. The phrase "symbolic structure" may sound exotic but it involves two familiar assumptions. First, authors give us versions of reality, artistic representations, not reality itself. Second, artistic representations are produced by means of codes, formulas, and literary traditions: they encode the stock expressions of a period, materials from which authors draw, and not necessarily in a slavish fashion. These codes are archives that hold beliefs, values, ideas about history, and modes of expression (or tropes) that are used to create systems that represent the social order to itself.

The frame stands between a vast, unlimited context or "general text" (Frow's term, 222) and the limited, linguistically enclosed literary text that employs symbolic structures. The frames that surround texts are mediating, discursive spaces because they include the discourses of academic analysis, of literary criticism, of readers' responses to the poem. The frames within texts that enclose symbolic structures or ideological systems are also discursive spaces. Each frame is a set of statements, written or spoken, in which power is negotiated, transferred, and manipulated in *inconspicuous* ways by the narrator and the characters.[11] Positioned between the order created by symbolic structures and the "real" order of social relations, the discourse of these textual frames also engages the audience and the author. Frames within the text parallel the outer frames that separate the text from Frow's "general text." Frames allow authors to transfer general text directly to written text by means of codes which author and audience share, and which, within the text, are shared by the narrator and his characters; thus frames are both barriers and points of contact and transference.

Symbolic systems not only create expectations about social roles and modes of existence but constitute the field of possibilities within which characters act: because symbolic systems expose the power relations of the social world, they help us understand how the characters are rendered as *subjects*. Literary texts relate general text (the "real" public world in which the characters exist) and symbolic content (the codes that govern private as well as public lives and that circumscribe them). Troilus's behavior as a young knight, for example, is not only a matter of his individual will or self-image, for it has been formed by his realization of the modes of behavior available to him as a Trojan aristocrat. That is, his behavior expresses his subjectivity, which is constituted by the world in which he lives. Criseyde's actions are likewise circumscribed—and far more tightly controlled—by the course of action both available *and* appropriate to her as a woman of a certain social and political standing; her possibilities, her self-image, and her understanding of her potential likewise express her subjectivity.

Symbolic systems are not naturally available alternatives. They do not owe their existence to nature but to tradition, which is the chief source of their power. To say that these systems are *symbolic* does not deny that they correspond to social realities but only emphasizes that they are ideological constructs imposed on society to give order, hierarchy, and the appearance of stability to social life. Part of a thesis—an assertion only, not a fact or a reality—about power and the people who use it, symbolic systems are at once both "mental images" of society and value systems. They are rhetorical figures which impose order on the world, establish hierarchical relations, and manage power. Chaucer creates all the frames within *Troilus and Criseyde* but not all the frames that enclose it. The frames within the poem can be seen as assertions that Chaucer understood and that, through his narrator, he posed as possibilities for the inhabitants of Troy. As we examine the correlation between those frames and the world of Chaucer's London, we discover the multiple indirect ways in which Chaucer's own history enters his story of Troy. Frames outside the poem include both those known to Chaucer (the framework of his courtly audience, for example) and those that began to multiply around the poem after his death.

What sorts of symbolic systems were available to Chaucer? One of the chief codes seen in *Troilus and Criseyde*—a notorious institution in the criticism of medieval literature—was *fin'amours*, usually called "the code of courtly love." Concerning this code, R. A.

Shoaf writes, "Its premise throughout was the sovereignty of the lady in amorous relations; . . . her sovereignty implied a chastening and a channelling of male aggression—hence also the marked civilizing tendency of *fin'amours* wherever it was followed."[12] If this code was a "channelling of male aggression," however, it also channelled female instincts, although in a more subtle way. It was a code that organized actions, propagandized certain virtues, and endorsed an ideal of public and private conduct. It was, therefore, a representational code, a means of demonstrating in texts a standard of ideal conduct that, as Chaucer and his characters frequently observe, had ceased to prevail.[13] The courtly love code, which stood at considerable variance from the social order of the fourteenth century, is really a cover for many codes that translate the order of society (the "general text") into symbolic terms and literary text.

In *Troilus and Criseyde*, Chaucer creates a woman who achieves the ultimate status in terms of the code. Virtually a goddess to Troilus, Criseyde stands in direct comparison to a "real" symbol, Pallas Athena, the goddess and protector of the city of Troy. Yet Criseyde loses her status in the symbolic order when, against her will and quite against the assurances of those in power, she is exchanged for Antenor, a warrior captured by the Greeks. The symbolic order, we shall see, always serves at the pleasure of the social order that creates, consumes, and controls it. Criseyde suffers this degradation at the height of her happiness as Troilus's lover: her triumph in the symbolic order of courtly love is undercut by her betrayal in the system of exchange that defines the political world. The social world, standing outside the frame, destroys the symbolic order that the frame protects.

The place of women who are within the symbolic system and who are framed by it (in several senses) is much discussed in Chaucer criticism. Several critics invoke Claude Lévi-Strauss's definition of culture as a relationship "between two groups of men [in which] the woman figures only as one of the objects in the exchange, and not as one of the partners."[14] "Woman is never anything but the locus of a more or less competitive exchange between two men, including the competition for the possession of mother earth," writes Luce Irigaray, who describes the issue succinctly.[15] For a symbol of "mother earth," Troy will do; for the competitive men, there are many choices, including the states of Troy and Greece, the leaders of their armies, Calkas (Criseyde's father) and Troilus, Troilus and Pandarus (her uncle and his best friend), and Troilus and Diomede (the Greek warrior who wins her in the end).

Although the social or "general text" can dominate symbolic structures, such structures can, in turn, dominate the social world in which they are perceived. Another symbolic system important to *The Canterbury Tales* but only briefly alluded to in *Troilus* is the medieval model according to which society was divided into three estates: those who prayed, those who fought, and those who worked. This model too was propagated as a response to social disorder and to threatening changes in social and economic systems; it too sought to contain violence. As Georges Duby shows, military violence preoccupied religious authorities who, during the early development of the tripartite structure (before 1200), feared the predatory powers of a newly empowered knightly class. The tripartite model emphasized that within the order of those who ruled, it was the king's responsibility to govern the military.[16] The model asserted the king's power by stressing the need for the military to serve and protect both church and state. Eventually, however, the control of violence of another kind, the social violence produced by economic exploitation between classes—especially those who ruled and those who worked—was also a concern, as we see in the Peasants' Rising of 1381. As a symbolic system, the trifunctional model rationalized the social system and, as the system began to change, supplied it with an image that naturalized competing social forces and met the need to keep inferior classes in their place with a social vision that stressed the interdependence rather than the competition of class interests.

A third symbolic system, implicit in both those already mentioned, is religion itself. Religious beliefs take many specific hierarchical forms (whether Western or Eastern). A pantheon of gods and goddesses or their equivalent deities superintend the material universe and its actions; a set of rules superintend the conduct of the faithful. Each religious system is arguably aimed at the preservation of social order (although that is not its only function, of course) and, if not at the outright control of violence, at the imposition of a hierarchy that ensures that violence, such as combat, is

40

directed to achieve acceptable and communal goals (including war). Symbolic systems interact with social systems and seek to maintain stability. It is the task of symbolic orders to maintain order, to rationalize the obvious inequalities of social life by framing them in images and words that ensure the survival of social systems. The trifunctional model, for example, found expression in two competing images: a three-legged stool, a figure that stressed interdependence; and the human body, a figure that hierarchized power relations and degraded labor as the lowest function.[17]

Symbolic orders are nothing if not grandiose in their attempts to demonstrate the inevitability of the structures they offer to the world. Writing of two medieval scholars and their knowledge of Macrobius's *Commentary on the Dream of Scipio*, Duby writes that they sought "to link the political order with the order of the stars."[18] Symbolic systems go so far as to invoke cosmic harmony in their search for analogies that frame social order. This example applies to Chaucer's use of *The Dream of Scipio* in *The Parliament of Fowls*, as I suggested in chapter 1; it also applies, even more specifically, to the cosmic order invoked at the end of *Troilus and Criseyde*.

What of less grandiose symbolic systems? One that is familiar to readers of this book is the academy, which employs a space we all know as a frame to maintain that system: the classroom. Within the classroom, both teachers and students occupy specific roles. The classroom frames a symbolic system that relates students to teachers in terms of formal codes, gestures, and so forth. The frame determines who sits where, who speaks and when, who is in charge, and who responds. There are numerous ways to alter and adapt those codes, but the adaptations (e.g., the teacher in jeans who sits in a circle with the class) acquire significance because they depart from a recognized norm—the more familiar expression of the order (e.g., the tweed-clad lecturer with a student audience). Within the symbolic order of the classroom, moreover, there is an institutional argument under way. There are assumptions about the student's dependence on the teacher that correlate with gender, age, social standing (class), and other factors.

Our perception of symbolic content depends on social context, on the social frame that encloses it. Aesthetic standards are not constant from culture to culture or period to period. Instead, the cultural space within which the frame is displayed is itself shifting and various, and when the symbolic order is rerepresented, or reframed, as we saw in the example of the toilet seat, its meaning changes. The shift from a nonaesthetic location to an aesthetic location does not alter the object but rather transforms its symbolic value. Just as physical structures serve as frames, as in the examples of the classroom and the art museum wall, literary texts also shape and define the symbolic systems they enclose. Each enclosure determines how that which is inside will be seen: each is a context in which an object or event is "quoted." To relate this concept to my example of the classroom as a frame, consider students and teachers who meet in other frames, such as a political rally, a bar, or a sports event: they are always conscious that the change in the frame corresponds to a shift in the places they occupy in the symbolic order. To relate this concept to *Troilus and Criseyde*, consider the resituating of lines from *Troilus and Criseyde* in the didactic treatise *Disce Mori*, a mid-fifteenth-century treatise for women, which quotes the first "Song" of Troilus (1.400–420) in a wholly Christian, didactic context.

A frame makes claims about its subject matter; it is not a neutral showcase. Instead, the frame asserts and makes arguments about symbolic structure, isolating symbolic systems that represent and refigure both the social worlds that texts describe and the worlds in which texts are written and read. By seeing the frame as an argument, we challenge authorial assertions—not from a hostile standpoint but from the premise that the author is always *doing something* with a text, not merely writing it. Likewise, the text is always *doing something* with its author and its readers. The text is an event, not a static thing; it is charged with ideological assertions about social life, art, history, and other ideas that the reader must discover and uncover.[19] Its ideological interests, concealed by the symbolic systems that express them, can be identified and analyzed as elements of the frame.

As the site of disruption and dislocation, the frame is a point at which social relations oppose and ultimately betray the symbolic order, as we see when Criseyde's symbolic significance to Troilus as a courtly lady is sacrificed to her significance in the public order of Troy. Chaucer disrupts his own frames, and not only to break "the fiction of spoken discourse" and call attention to the text as "a

42

written thing."[20] Some frames present Trojan politics, wars, and love affairs as analogous to those of Chaucer's time. These frames suggest that readers in London and characters in Troy share systems: they pray to divinities (even the same ones), fear enemies, and celebrate victories. But these similarities are undermined when the narrator denounces Trojan symbolic systems and asserts English values against them.

Such frames are structures installed in the text by the author and activated by the reader. Chaucer frames each of the first four books of *Troilus and Criseyde* with a prologue—an address to readers in book 1, an elaborate proem in each of the next three books—that isolates certain issues within each book. In book 5 he employs a reverse structure, an epilogue that imposes multiple frames to close the text. The structure of the books can also be seen as the narrator's framing of parallel scenes or his framing of actions within architectural frames such as temples, windows, and city walls that have acquired symbolic force in the text.[21] But the narrator also frames more explicitly by reacting to certain episodes and telling us how to value them. And characters perform in an analogous way, constructing fields within which actions and speeches are interpreted. Readers will disagree about the significance of such structural divisions but will not, I hope, dispute their usefulness in underscoring specific features of the text.

My chief focus is on internal frames, which mark structural divisions and features within texts and also configure the social world within texts in terms of enclosures. The love affair between Troilus and Criseyde is framed by its courtly social context; the shared values of that circle include the ties of family (the brotherhood of Troilus and Hector, for example), which are in turn framed by the parliamentary forum in which the lovers' personal desires, the basis of Hector's defense of Criseyde even without knowing about her attachment to his brother, are subject to new pressures. The parliament is in turn framed by the larger public whose wishes it must heed; and the city is framed by its wall of defense against the Greeks. The war itself is framed by the many tellings of it that the narrator points to as he wraps yet another frame of his own making around it.

Such frames are more than successive layers, and this is the point at which analogies between frames in narrative art and the frames that surround sketches and other art work begins to break down. Narrative frames do more than enclose their subjects. Each narrative frame has a different focus; each frame has a different center. Sometimes readers are able to discover the center or focus of an existing frame only by imposing a new frame on it. That is one way in which, to quote Frow, frames serve to disrupt the "interiority" of the work and betray "the *interest* by which it [the work] is delimited" (Frow, 219). External frames, produced—and disrupted—by readers outside the world of the text, also betray interest. External frames are both social and literary. They include institutional frameworks, such as the "major author" and the "literary canon," and critical frameworks that reveal the ends to which we put our work with texts and how, as we read and write, we frame and reframe the conditions in which we read. A significant example is the way in which some feminist critics have disrupted the traditional idea of Chaucer as a representative poet by stressing the exclusive values of his work. The revisionism undertaken by such reframing seems to have a plainly social purpose in exposing masculine suppressions of the feminine.

The reading that follows frames the text in several ways. Within the twofold limit of the frame I have discussed above—that is, internal and external—I have selected a framing character or force as the means of organizing my discussion of each of the poem's five books. Book 1 is framed by the narrator, book 2 by Pandarus: this is a correspondence that has become traditional in the criticism, a pairing of shaping forces outside and inside the poem. Book 3 is seen within the frame of the Boethian concept of universal love introduced in the proem and often referred to in the text. Book 4 is framed by war, which overshadows the love between Paris and Helen and ends the love between Troilus and Criseyde. Book 5 is framed by fate.

My use of the frame approaches the text in terms of both social and symbolic orders. The line that divides these systems is problematic, unstable, and difficult to locate. For the frame disappears into the work (into the literary text) and into the general text, the work's nonaesthetic context. Frow writes, "But the mere fact of the convergence of the internal structure and the contextual function of the text at the 'edge' of the text indicates that the frame does not simply separate an outside from an inside but unsettles the dis-

tinction between the two" (Frow, 223). The work that is framed is
the viewer's focus, and the frame tends to "sink into" or become
part of the work, as a movie becomes part of the screen and a text
becomes the book that frames it. It is especially difficult to see
frames in literary texts, for, as Frow writes, "We have been taught
to naturalize the space of the aesthetic object, to lose ourselves in
an inside which is as unlimited as the world, and this means that
our 'natural' inclination is to see the work in the same way we see
the world, without awareness of the edge of our eyes' scan" (Frow,
224). Frow compares the frame to the line dividing morning from
night—a line we know about only because we see a difference
between two kinds of space. We see light or darkness, not the line
dividing (framing) them. Thus the frame can be insubstantial, operative but unseen at the point at which it decided difference. Thus
we must, as Frow says, "force" attention to the frame.

Frames are already in place and operative before we realize
their presence, so it is not easy to detect or "force" attention to their
work. It is, we often think, the purpose of the frame to lead the eye
to art *at first without our seeing the frame*, which should be observed only secondarily, if it has done its job effectively. Thus the
frame has already engaged and manipulated us before the frame itself is evaluated. It is important to detect the frame because the
frame is not a neutral force that is simply "there," surrounding a
text. We will see the importance of this statement about the usefulness of symbolic orders when we identify the frames used to enclose *Troilus and Criseyde*: the tension between the real and the
symbolic implies that the symbolic is in the service of the real, just
as the representation of sexual life in the "code of courtly love" can
be seen both as an innocent flattery of women and as a code preserving social distinctions and forms of order outside texts and
thus keeping women at a disadvantage. The social frame of our own
reading can also be difficult to identify; it too does its work without
being detected.

If frames manipulate us, of course, we also manipulate them.
The frame can always be framed. To read a text in terms of its
frames is to link a method of the reader's own to the text, so that
one reads self-consciously at all times. The frame of method reminds us that the text operates on us, just as we operate on it: our
method tells us, quite literally, what the text is good for. The frame

brings us to "the formal and institutional conditions of reading," writes Frow,[22] and it is important to remember, whatever the pleasures of the text, that reading is institutionalized for us in culture and that the next step, once we have read, is to act on our reading.

5

Past and Present:
Book 1 and the Narrator

The "double sorwe of Troilus" dominates the poem's opening stanza, but the emphasis in the first 60 lines is not on Troilus, Troy, or even on the world of lovers, happy and unhappy, whom the narrator serves. It is on the narrator himself, who stands between the lovers of the past and the lovers in his audience, between ancient love and new love. He is himself a frame dividing these worlds, a barrier but also a sounding board. His role as an apologist for love is complicated by contradictions in phenomena he describes: love past and present, religion then and now, social worlds public and private. In book 1 he seeks to reconcile these oppositions.

The narrator begins by evoking the poem's ending, and the reader follows his lead, looking to the poem's conclusion at the very outset. The grim declarations that open *Troilus and Criseyde* are soon forgotten once the plot gets under way, but the proems that open the second, third, and fourth books contain ever-darker invocations to the Muses, and Thesiphone, one of the three Furies, makes her appearance in the sixth line of the first book. In contrast to these foreboding references, appeals to the Christian God balance classical tragedy with Christian hope. Before 30 lines have passed, the narrator asks his audience, "ye loveres, that bathen in gladnesse" (1.22),[1] to pray for unhappy lovers, including Troilus, so that love will bring him to heaven. He asks that they pray "to God so dere" for himself and his narrative skills (1.32), for those who are slandered in love, hoping that "God, for his benignite," will grant them an early death (1.40–41), and for happy lovers, hoping that God's "ay good perseveraunce" will keep them safe (1.44). He will write about the woe of lovers and have compassion for them as if he were their brother (1.47–51). The narrator alternates between the classical, pre-Christian world of Troy and the world of Christ's death and resurrection, which by implication is the Christian world of Chaucer's own time. Although, as the narrator says at the start of book 2, "in sondry londes, sondry ben usages," and "ecch contree hath his lawes" (2.28, 2.42), we also know that in spite of such differences, lovers in the past "spedde as wel in love as men now do" (2.26). The introduction seals these two perspectives, demonstrating that lovers then and lovers now (the narrator included) are much the same. Or are they? For as long as the poem holds its ancient subject and its readers together on that shared horizon, *Troilus and Criseyde* retains its immediacy. But at the end of the work the poet allows the horizons to pull apart, creating a new perspective as the story retreats and finally shrinks to the dismal status awarded ancient examples of unhappy fate in love.

The shift to an exclusively Christian perspective at the end of book 5, often regarded as a turnabout on the narrator's part, actually is elaborately prepared for by frequent vacillations between these two ethical realms—these two ethical frames—throughout the preceding books. The narrator refuses to establish a single perspective. Given that the same behavior looks very different in a classical as opposed to a Christian frame, this refusal significantly destabilizes our response to the poem. With our sympathy engaged but its basis unsettled, the narrator goes "streght to my matere," which is "the double sorwes here / Of Troilus, in lovynge of Criseyde" (1.54–55), a return to his first line.

The narrator has already moved through several narrative levels, addressing ethics, history, politics, and sexual love. All levels afford him opportunities to compare customs then with customs now, past with present. The historical is one of the largest but, curiously, also the least visible frames of the poem. We are reminded in every book that Troy is at war, but the war seems to be part of the background rather than the center of the plot. The frame of political conflict, although fully submerged in the text, is a frame that both enhances the love story and works against it.

Two frames, that of Troy and that of the history to which the Troy legend belongs, are already operating in the poem's first lines. As C. David Benson shows, Chaucer did much both to emphasize the antiquity of the setting and to suggest its similarities to London.[2] There are reasons to compare Troy, the poem's setting, to London, Chaucer's setting for performing it. But the comparison between a weak and self-absorbed Troy losing a war and a weak London divided in its leadership is barely implied, and the "pertinent lessons" (Benson, *Chaucer's "Troilus,"* 71) said to be created by the comparison are not obvious. Although, at the most general level, "New Troy" can be held responsible for avoiding the errors of the old and so enlarging on its glories, it is not clear that any of these comparisons is fundamentally important or sufficiently appropriate to justify an elaborate reading of Troy as Chaucer's London. Troy was important as a narrative of England's origins, but full appreciation of the political usefulness of the legend seems to have awaited the reign of Henry V, who commissioned both John Lydgate's massive version of Troy's history (in 1412) and a deluxe copy of Chaucer's poem. To Lydgate, however, it was the warrior Achilles, not the lover Troilus, who mattered most, and Benson himself notes that Lydgate's work does not claim "that Troy has special moral advice to offer its descendants" (Benson, *History*, 118).

A brief look at Chaucer's handling of historical sources will suggest why his use of Troy does not underscore the fourteenth-century context of the poem. We saw, in chapter 1, that Chaucer is regarded as a "classicizer." If he "classicized"—that is, succeeded in portraying as "timeless"—his own age, Chaucer also "classicized" the Trojan past. Janet Coleman describes "classicizing" as the dependence of medieval vernacular literatures on classical Latin literature for "corroborative source and inspiration" (Coleman, 46). *Troilus and Criseyde* shows us how he uses various sources to corroborate his tale. The poem is a translation of Boccaccio's *Il Filostrato*, of which Chaucer may have had a French translation. The poem is also indebted to Dante's *Divine Comedy* and to *The Romance of the Rose*.[3] Chaucer also used histories of Troy by early authors, whom he knew through late medieval commentators, including Joseph of Exeter.[4] The mixture of Trojan histories unsettles written authority. The narrator shifts his attitude, sometimes saying that he cannot follow his sources but at other times referring the reader to these same sources for further details. "The historical is thus invoked," Richard Rambuss writes of the place of Troy in *The Book of the Duchess*, "but only in the service of the private concerns of love."[5] This observation applies to *Troilus and Criseyde* equally well. Chaucer's treatment of sources allows his narrator's personal interpretation of them to triumph over the impersonal, ancient authority of other versions of the legend. One result is to elevate the personal, constituted by the immediate world of the poet and his audience, to the level of the public, constituted by the past and its authorities. Another result is to obscure the political relevance of issues raised by the text. Throughout the poem, the historical subject of Troy waivers before the narrator's reliance on his sources and his inventive departures from them.

Troilus and Criseyde takes place amid a violent conflict that began with a violent act of love. The Greeks have besieged Troy for ten years, "the ravysshyng to wreken of Eleyne" (1.62)—and that violence will soon end a love that begins in its midst. The war motivates the first important act in the poem, significantly a betrayal. "A gret devyn" who is named Calkas (1.66) has learned from the Delphic oracle (Apollo Delphicus) "by sort" (that is, by divination) that Troy will be destroyed. Calkas's discovery is made in secret, and the secrecy with which he acts on it, leaving the city, is emphasized: "ful pryvely / He stal anon" (1.80–81). Calkas stands between two worlds, which he both divides as a traitor and bridges as a visionary. He is a framing force in the poem, and his prophecy is influential—the Greeks believe him. But the narrator devotes little discursive space to it. Because we are not aware of how the vision is interpreted but rather learn only what its import is, Calkas's mediating function has little fictional significance.

When his departure is discovered, Calkas is denounced. His betrayal is a scandal whose most immediate effect is to cast suspicion on his daughter, Criseyde, a widow without a confidant, a "hevenyssh perfit creature" (1.104) who is now endangered. The citizens of Troy declare their outrage and insist that "al his kyn atones / Ben worthi for to brennen, fel and bones" (1.91). Frightened at this development, Criseyde appeals to Hector's mercy. The elder brother of Troilus, Hector adjudicates the political controversies of the city. He promises to protect both Criseyde's honor and her body and to ensure that her status—what I call her "symbolic value"—will remain as it was when her father was in Troy.

In only a few stanzas the narrator has shifted from the political landscape of the Trojan War to the personal world to which the poem is largely confined. He demonstrates the social worlds, great and small, through which the plot weaves: alliances of power, realized either as personal relationships or wars between nations; communications both intimate and public; and the human relationships of blood, friendship, and love that support and sustain these conflicts. These constraints confine the lovers' actions in three different circles. The first circle is that of family relationships: Pandarus is Criseyde's uncle; Troilus is the son of Priam, the king, and brother to Hector. The second is the circle of nobles, a close and concerned community, as we see in book 2 when Pandarus alarms them by spreading rumors about Criseyde. The third is a large, impersonal circle of national and political alliances. It is in the realm of family relationships that the lovers become most free and are most indulged. When moving in other circles they become more restricted; in the third circle they are especially confined by the social demands that shape their public identities and the pressures those demands create on their interior, individual selves. The events of *Troilus and Criseyde* force constant negotiation between the social and the individual, the private and the public.

Criseyde is less free in each circle than is her lover. Her world is controlled by men in powerful positions: Calkas, Hector, Pandarus, and Troilus all influence her fate and help manage her life, for each man connects her to a different kind of social order. Calkas is a high priest who participates in supernatural, secret realms and the public world of Troy, bringing state religion and politics to bear upon her familial identity. Pandarus functions within both familial and political units. Related to Criseyde and friend to Troilus, he is a prominent figure at the court and is therefore also a bridge between public and private worlds. Although he is a king's son and a valiant warrior, Troilus is seen predominantly within the secret world of his own thoughts. He is particularly susceptible to self-doubt and indecision, and some readers delight in mocking his passivity. But this response ignores the meaning of his position between desire and destiny. Hector, his brother, by contrast appears only slightly concerned with the pri-

51

vate realm; he seems to function as the public half of Troilus's consciousness.

Much of the poem's energy is concentrated on the circles of family and nobility; little is spent on the larger political circle until book 4. Thus, just as the situational framework supported by the narrator "sinks" into the text, dropping from sight (even though it continues to function), the concerns of state and religion also tend to merge into the text and disappear. They too sometimes surface unexpectedly, as in book 4 when the citizens of Troy vigorously endorse the proposal that Criseyde leave the city as part of a prisoner exchange with the Greeks. The social pressures of public politics are sketchy throughout, but they erupt into the narrative at a moment's notice, a sure sign that they are always present.

Recent readers have emphasized the consequences of these male-centered social worlds for Criseyde, who is frequently seen as an overpowered, defenseless victim of circumstances. At the same time, her disadvantages in the social order are compensated for by her status in the symbolic order. In the various symbolic systems of the poem, the woman's position is celebrated, protected, and highly valued. Her father is a high priest; she is often referred to as a goddess, and even before the love affair begins the narrator comments that she was sent to earth "in scornynge of nature" (1.105), as though she were divine rather than human. Pandarus admires her as his niece even as he exploits her through the superior familial position he occupies as an elder male. In offering her protection, Hector assures Criseyde that her status will remain high. Hector thus underscores an independence which is, as his later actions make clear, more symbolic than socially valid. To Troilus as a courtly lover, of course, Criseyde comes to stand for everything on the symbolic level. In the end, however, he declares that she stands for nothing.

These contradictions are possible because the poem operates on two levels of value, the symbolic and the social, that are almost mirror images of each other. The sexual role that is constrained within the social is valorized in the symbolic. In the case of the symbolic order of courtly love, David Aers suggests that valorization is compensation for the fundamental inequality of relations in the social order of the sexes. Aers points out that the courtly code stood at considerable variance from the social order of the fourteenth

century. The woman who was seen as all-powerful in the symbolic
order was, in the social order, virtually powerless, while the male
whose aggression was tamed in the symbolic order retained the
freedom to exercise his strength. Such a woman might have been
adored, but she was not very free. Indeed, Aers argues that women
were worshiped in terms of the symbolic order as compensation for
their oppression in real social relations.[6]

What is true for Criseyde is true in reverse for Troilus. He generally appears to be a powerful agent whose freedom is severely
constrained by a love affair he must keep secret. Yet the symbolic
order keeps Criseyde in her place without restraining Troilus's aggression. Indeed, just as Calkas and Hector gain status when they
act within the symbolic order, Troilus's status as a lover enhances
his prowess as a warrior. Thus the male figures seem to triumph in
both symbolic and social spheres, on both sides of the frame, even
when, within the symbolic order, they supposedly serve the
woman's wishes.

Relations within the social and symbolic worlds are unequal,
and preserving this imbalance requires that the relations not be
scrutinized too closely. Such inspection is made more difficult because the relations are kept secret. The symbolic order is enclosed
by secrecy and silence; the symbolic order is betrayed when that
silence is broken. Calkas's reason for deserting Troy is a secret
between him and the gods that he shares only with the Greeks.
When his disappearance "generally was spoken" by the Trojans
(1.86), Criseyde's social position (as well as his own) is redefined.
She is forced to speak—to ask for Hector's mercy. When she ob-
tains it, she regains a secure place in the symbolic order and returns home to hold "hir stille," a retreat into silence (1.126). The
opposition between speech and silence, between public knowledge
and private circumstance, comes to define her affair with Troilus.
Public knowledge of their liaison would have prevented the exchange that separates them at the end of the poem; they preserve
secrecy and protect the symbolic order, but eventually the social
foundations of their union erode. Even if Troilus were to claim her
and insist that she remain in Troy, their happiness could not out-
weigh the political demand that she be exchanged.

In his opening stanzas the narrator completes the paradigm
within which Criseyde operates: her weaknesses, seen in her vul-

nerability to gossip and dependency on authority, are offset by her strengths, including her understanding that she can deploy speech and silence to serve her own interests. In her brief appearance in the social world of book 1, Criseyde shows herself to be politically astute and discreet. Her understanding of social connections as the flow of cause and effect contrasts with Troilus's desire for a world that does not change. That contrast appears in the next few stanzas, in which the gradations of her behavior are implicitly contrasted with his turnabout as he veers from a deep hostility toward love, from an attitude that emphasizes his strength and independence to an idealized perspective in which love rules all, including him. His transition from the social to the symbolic, from the order in which he dominates to the order in which he is dominated, is absolute.

It is the social rather than the military side of Trojan life that draws the narrator. He impatiently refers his audience to other sources if they want to read about the war, and then, having reminded us of these great events on the periphery, reports that war or no, the Trojans do not forgo their traditions. The feast to which the narrator turns is a religious festival honoring "Palladion" (1.153), the goddess Pallas Athena, on whom Troy's safety depends. Fundamental to the social order of the city, Pallas is an icon in which the social and the symbolic converge, a goddess of great symbolic importance both to Criseyde—another goddess—and to the poem. The statue of Pallas honored at this feast is later stolen by Antenor, the Trojan warrior for whom Criseyde is exchanged in book 5. At this feast Troilus meets a goddess of his own. Dante first sees Beatrice in a church, as Petrarch first sees Laura.[7] And, as Paris views Helen, Troilus first sees his mistress in a temple, where she stands "ful lowe and stille allone," staying behind others "undre shames drede." Yet Criseyde carries a "ful assured lokyng and manere" (1.178, 1.180, 1.182). The combination of attributes—modesty and silence with self-possession—reinforces the impression created by Criseyde's first act in the poem.

In this setting, in which Criseyde's maturity has already been demonstrated, Troilus appears to be a young fool who is overly eager to disparage men who sigh for beautiful ladies (1.202). This blasphemy against the god of love stirs the god to revenge: he shoots Troilus with his bow (1.209–210). The narrator makes no apology for this act; instead, he elaborates on the consequences in the language of fate and fortune. Troilus does not yet realize that he who rises must descend, a lesson Criseyde has obviously learned already. The hero is degraded in an extended comparison between his own independence and that of a horse: the horse may be proud of his appearance but knows he is "but an hors, and horses lawe / I moot endure, and with my feres drawe" (1.223–24). That is, even the horse knows that however handsome, he is limited by his nature and subject to the laws of nature; thus he must share the burden borne by others of his kind. Troilus has controverted this natural law, refusing to recognize that he is like his "feres." The narrator then underscores the lesson with an address to "ye wise, proude, and worthi folkes alle," who should not scorn love, as Troilus has, or forget that they are bound by the "lawe of kynde," which even Bayard the horse understands (1.232–38). This discussion continues for another 20 lines in which the narrator encourages lovers to submit to the bonds of love, since love has often made lovers happier. This rather bland encouragement, which moves effortlessly from past to present, works against the complex assertions of the opening lines, the "bidding prayers" (1.22–56) in which both happy and disappointed lovers appear. The end of the poem also undercuts these simplistic associations between then and now. The address to lovers ends with a self-conscious reference to the "joie" and "cares colde" of love (1.264), after which the narrator returns to Troilus.

This disjunction, the making of frames, is a hallmark of the work. One way to gauge the intensity of the text, and to isolate points at which the narrator redefines his connection to it, is to mark off the shifts from a temporal, causal framework, in which the narrative describes rational human causality, to a universalized frame larger than human causes, a static and unchanging perspective that dwarfs earthly activity. We will see this double frame invoked in various dreams later in the poem. On the one hand, events are made to seem temporal and to result from human causes; this is the perspective that Criseyde maintains. On the other, events are not transparently responsive to human desires but are out of their control and in the hands of fate or fortune; this is the perspective the hero prefers. As he appraises the women in the temple, noting which are "of town," presumably better connected than others, Troilus's eye falls on Criseyde "upon cas" (by chance), piercing a crowd "til on Criseyde it smot, and ther it stente" (1.270–73). He immediately checks his response: the scorner of love cannot afford to be affected by love, at least not in public. The need for silence thwarts speech and action. He is transfixed by her rather haughty appearance ("which somdel deignous was," 1.290); her gaze overpowers him, for therein love dwells. Troilus's hostility to love is vanquished; the narrator intones, "Blissed be Love, that kan thus folk converte!" (1.308).

Stricken, but not quite fully stunned ("nat fullich al awhaped," 1.316), Troilus returns home, working to dissimulate his love, lest he be charged with hypocrisy. He dismisses his retinue and enters into the first of his many private meditations, solitary moments that constitute the most private world of the text, a world wherein the public worlds of the text are recreated. In this passage, Troilus operates as a framer, discoursing on his experience and articulating the problematic transition from scorner to lover. Like others who frame, he finds the point of transition difficult to locate and yet impossible to deny. Troilus has expressed his last living contempt for love; converted to its powers, he will periodically chide himself for having fallen into slavery, but he is now as rigidly defined within it as he defined himself against it just a short time ago. We learn to associate Troilus with permanence by noting the mental process through which he configures and internalizes images of Criseyde. When he was in the temple, the desire created by her look was so great that "in his herte botme gan to stiken / Of hir his fixe and depe impressioun" (1.297–98). Now, in his chamber, he consults this image—"that he wel koude in his herte fynde" (1.367)—and hopes that if he serves her properly he will be accepted into her graces or, failing that, will be able to pass for one of her servants (1.371). The narrator adds that "travaille nor grame / Ne myghte for so goodly oon be lorn / As she" (1.372–74). Troilus imagines that no work or pain would be lost if it were dedicated to one so beautiful; but if he were discovered, knowledge of his devotion would only bring credit to both of them (they would be "up-born / Of alle lovers wel more than biforn," 1.375–76).

Here we see that the narrator acknowledges the complexity of social orders even as he writes about only one. Troilus imagines that neither labor nor suffering would be lost on one so fine as

Criseyde. This self-serving moment is undercut by the narrator's comment that the knight was "ful unavysed of his woo comynge" (1.378). Troilus intends to pursue her secretly, however, for he knows the importance of keeping the affair quiet. Love "to wide yblowe," he knows, is sweet seed that will produce bitter fruit (1.384–85). We also see why differentiations of class are not, ultimately, significant in this poem: the concept of labor and the status of work are utterly symbolic, without correspondence to the social worlds of production and consumption. Because labor has a symbolic presence only, a textual reference alone cannot draw attention to the inequality of production and consumption in the social world.

Troilus thus assumes the guise of the courtly lover. His actions subsequent to his first glimpse of Criseyde show that he understands and subscribes to the symbolic order as a code of conduct for lovers. The concern for secrecy, the desire to offer constant, even debasing service, the need to suffer for love and finally to sing about it: Troilus checks off these items from a mental list. He knows what he is supposed to be doing: he understands the rules of the private world he wants to create within the public world he cannot leave. Troilus's first song (showing Chaucer's debt to Petrarch, sonnet 88[8]) sets forth a list of contraries between which the lover stands—"O quike deth, O swete harm so queynte" (1.411), and so forth. One of these images supplies a motif that operates for the entire poem: Troilus sees himself "Al stereless withinne a boot," "amydde the see, bitwixen wyndes two, / That in contrarie stonden evere mo" (1.416–18). Later Troilus longs to be "aryved in the port / Of deth" (1.526–27); still later he all but drowns in his own "salte teres" (1.543), in the sea of his sorrows.[9]

At the end of the song Troilus pledges himself to the god of love who dwells in Criseyde's eyes. His royal birth does not isolate him from love's power, and when he thinks about love he begins to neglect everything else. With this slightly comic and certainly unflattering impression, the narrator draws our attention to the frame, where he pauses to acknowledge the experience of those in his audience who understand what Troilus is learning: that "the ner [the fire] he was, the more he brende" (1.448–49). This is the first of many descriptions of Troilus manifesting love's pathology—the sickness that befalls those who fall in love—and another of the poem's courtly commonplaces. Yet the results of this private weakness are transformed in public behavior: Troilus has never been a more valiant fighter than he is now that he is in love; his public role is reinterpreted in terms of his passion for Criseyde. He "dide ek swich travaille / In armes, that to thenke it was merveille" (1.475–76). But his motive has nothing to do with patriotism or public allegiance; rather, he fights so that Criseyde will like him better because of his fame (1.481). It is important to see how, as he operates within the symbolic system of courtly love, Troilus enhances his status in the social world: the symbolic order and the social order both work to his advantage, for love only increases his aggression as a warrior.

Troilus's extreme emotions—his weeping, his depression, and his habit of taking to his bed to writhe in the miseries of unrequited love—have inspired much contempt among readers. Students are often incredulous at such "unmasculine" conduct, and their teachers sometimes find that "courtly love" fails to account for the hero's excesses. It is significant that Chaucer's idea of a man's conduct in this situation is more flexible than that of modern viewers. Chaucer allows Troilus his tears and frequently mentions (although he rarely illustrates) his valor on the battlefield. The narrator also periodically chides the hero's excesses and even allows Troilus to mock himself ("O fool, now artow in the snare!" [1.507]). Now that he has joined the dance of love, Troilus understands his vulnerability to criticism. At one point he fears exposure and seems to prefer death to public ridicule, but he immediately asks both God and his lady for mercy and for some sign to reward him (1.533–35).

The hero's state now fully demonstrated, the narrator introduces the third major character, Pandarus, who also negotiates two worlds but who is the only character that the narrator eventually sacrifices to shallow pragmatism. Pandarus, to whom the narrator will soon hand off his framing function, finds Troilus weeping and peppers Troilus with questions. Is his misery caused by fear of the Greeks, or by a sudden conversion that causes him to regret his sins? Pandarus tries to bully Troilus into some display of courage and self-possession (1.564), but Troilus denies the allegations of fear and refuses to tell Pandarus why he weeps: "I hide it for the beste," he says (1.581). Troilus eventually explains that he has fallen in love but does not indicate with whom. When Pandarus presses for details, Troilus repeats his earlier wish to sail into the port of death (1.606). Pandarus replies that the blind can go where those with sight cannot, and that "a fool may ek a wis man ofte gide" (1.630), no great flattery to himself of course, who intensifies the comparison when he says sharp tools need blunt instruments in order to remain sharp: "By his contrarie is every thyng declared" (1.637). Pandarus articulates the oppositions that have already appeared in Troilus's first song and that recur throughout the text. (The patterns of contraries, like those of the ship and other figurative motifs, are expressed in all the voices of the poem.)

Pandarus supplies a highly and, indeed, oddly topical example at this point: he refers to Paris and the shepherdess Oënone, whom Paris deserted when he took Helen, thus calling to mind the faithlessness of the man whose rape of Helen began the Trojan War (1.654). Taking after the narrator, who commented on the inadequacy of his own experience as a lover, Pandarus fabricates a story about himself, claiming to be in love with one who ignores him and so qualifying as one who can advise Troilus (1.674). He would not discourage Troilus even if it were Helen that Troilus loved, an offensive suggestion that passes here without objection. Pandarus's curiosity about Troilus's love is mixed with a distinctive philosophy of love (his own code), proverbs, and pragmatism. He labors to break down the hero's resistance to public knowledge of his love, assuring Troilus that to include him in the secret would be to retain its privacy while relieving Troilus of a burden. Understandably Troilus barely reacts to these shoddy arguments and false postures (1.723–25), and Pandarus compares him to a Boethian ass who hears the sound of the harp but no melody—that is, it is as if Troilus takes in only the noise of Pandarus's speech, not its wisdom (1.730–35).[10]

Remembering that "Man maketh ofte a yerde / With which the maker is hymself ybeten" (1.740–41), Troilus remains silent, debating the importance of secrecy—the demand of the code, and, equally important, the shield of his vulnerability as a converted scorner of love. He dismisses the proverbs and insists that he cannot be cured and will die (1.758). Pandarus replies with another proverb—fools delight in their woe and do not seek remedy for it (1.762–63)—and offers to tell the lady, since Troilus himself is afraid to. Troilus refuses the offer, saying that the lady could never love such a wretch as he (1.777). Pandarus refutes this claim first by ridiculing its despairing outlook and then by saying that a man who refuses to act on his love because of "coward herte" is indeed contemptible: "What womman koude loven swich a wrecche?" (1.798). She may well think that he died for fear of the Greeks rather than for love of her. Here again the war serves merely as a pretext for ignoble comparisons, a foil for the symbolic order of love, rather than—as it becomes later—a devastating threat to it.

Pandarus mixes courtly commonplaces with his folklore and proverbs. Even a love scorned for 20 years should not despair, he advises (1.811–15); the knight should always be ready to serve his lady. This idealized appeal to courtly devotion calls to mind the experience of Palamon and Arcite in "The Knight's Tale," in which years pass between the moment in which they fall in love with Emily and the first opportunity either has to speak a single word to her, and the view of the first of the three eagles in *The Parliament of Fowls*.[11] Pandarus, the great pragmatist, has assumed the voice of a lover, a voice and identity that Troilus recognizes as his own. Thus persuaded, Troilus surrenders his secret. Pandarus, having feigned a presence in the symbolic order, has not only gained the confidence of his friend in the social order but established a coidentity with him. Criseyde constitutes a social bond between the men, another of the many ways in which she acquires value by serving as a medium of exchange. We already know that she mediates a tension between the Trojans and the Greeks; later we see that she is frequently defined by her role as third party to two others. Hereafter, until nearly the end of the poem, Pandarus and Troilus share the joys and sorrows of the love affair and form a homosocial (not necessarily homosexual) bond. Their relationship becomes more intimate, it is true, but the social system ensures that their proximity is mediated by a woman whom both admire and whom one loves. Indeed, their relationship seems to demand her role in it, as though an unmediated connection between the two men would be unthinkable without the woman as its ostensible object.[12] Thus, as the frame in book 2, Pandarus mediates structures between Criseyde and Troilus with his words and inventions; but his mediation is supplemented by Criseyde's role as a medium for the two men. I return to these issues of homosocial bonding, and their implications for men's language, in my conclusion.

When Troilus denounces Fortune as his foe, Pandarus replies that Fortune treats everyone alike; one should not forget that "as hire joies moten overgon, / So mote hire sorwes passen everechon" (1.846–47). Here is a startling reversal of Boethian wisdom. Boethius describes how Lady Philosophy tells Boethius that no man can ever be secure until he has been forsaken by Fortune, for until then the two-faced nature of the goddess is not known to him (Boethius, book 2, prose 3). Once having fallen into misfortune, this man is therefore free and knows not to trust Fortune again. Pandarus takes the opposite view and encourages the downcast Troilus to hope for an upturn in his fortunes. He who will be cured, says Pandarus, invoking another commonplace, must first show his wound (this too is from Boethius, book 1, prose 4–5). Pandarus will see to it that Troilus wins his lady, even if she turns out to be Pandarus's sister (1.861); once again, Pandarus's callous references to procuring women degrades Troilus's status as an idealized lover. When Pandarus announces, "Here bygynneth game" (1.868), his participation in the affair is no longer vicarious. He is now both in the picture and around it.

When Troilus says that his "swete fo" is Criseyde, Pandarus praises her, recalls Troilus's earlier scorn of love, and demands that he confess to the god of love and repent his earlier attitudes (1.932–34). Pandarus catechizes him in devotion to the god of love, takes charge of the affair, and becomes the poem's architect. Pandarus has reason to be confident, for Criseyde is his niece. Immediately after revealing this familial tie, Pandarus invokes the symbolic system of religious belief, saying that all are subject either to divine or to earthly love ("Celestial, or elles love of kynde" [979]). Criseyde is not yet ready for divine love, although she is worthy of it; she will, he hopes, follow the "law of kynde" and become Troilus's. And if she will not love Troilus, "a worthi knyght," Pandarus will "holde it for a vice" (1.986–87). These lines represent Criseyde as bound by several ties, social as well as symbolic; familial, religious, and natural constraints render her vulnerable to Pandarus. Now that Troilus has been converted, Pandarus predicts that he will become love's strongest supporter (1.1000). Troilus immediately turns to the likelihood of Pandarus's success and asks if a niece would want to hear such things from her own uncle (1.1022). Undaunted, Pandarus replies with a pun: he will hear nothing of such "nyce fare," foolish business (1.1025), and Troilus should let him work as he will. Troilus then submits to Pandarus, swearing to fight the Greeks with new vigor. "My lif, my deth, hol in thyn hond I leye," he says (1.1053), a pledge Pandarus warmly returns.

When he leaves the chamber, however, Pandarus's thoughts descend rapidly from the chivalric heights of plighting "trowthe" and turn quickly to the practical matter of telling Criseyde about Troilus's love. The book closes with an architectural metaphor that reveals Pandarus as the central shaper of the text hereafter, planning his project with his "hertes line" (imaginary line, 1.1068). Troilus, in the meanwhile, revived, is again seen as the vigorous, victorious knight that Chaucer never lets far from view. His reputation in Troy flourishes: he "gat hym so in grace, / That ecch hym loved that loked on his face" (1.1077–78). Still wounded but a bit relieved, Troilus surrenders to Pandarus, who will "dryeth forth his aventure" (1.1092).

The figure of Pandarus as a builder is a powerful reference to the frame in a common usage of Middle English: that is, to frame is to build, as to "frame in" a house, to frame an argument, and so forth. Chaucer, interestingly, uses the expression only once (3.530)—in reference to Pandarus. We see how effectively Pandarus, used here to register the distinct social powers of family and friendship, isolates and then bridges the worlds separating the lovers. He does so through fictions—through lies, white and otherwise—designed to ensnare his niece and rationalize the desires of his friend. Pandarus is himself a frame who alternately imposes himself on Criseyde as family and on Troilus as a friend. First he stands protectively over his niece, serving as a barrier against exposure and exploitation. Then he poses aggressively as he tries to undermine the very defenses he (quite literally) mans. Pandarus manipulates these frames of his own devising carefully; he "caste his werk ful wisely or he wroughte" (1.1071).

The narrator has steered the tale between past and present, looking now at Troy and now at his immediate audience, invoking Christian belief as he describes pagan customs, switching from the vast context of the Trojan War to the immediate, private world of sexual love. His efforts to mediate these differences are irresolute. The play of authorities and the tensions thus established will eventually have to be arrested and resolved. But that work remains for the conclusion, when the narrator, having occupied us with a love story that calls for pre-Christian ethics, insists that only Christian ethics are important. The narrator is, as a frame, superseded after book 1, although he intrudes into all the books, periodically, to unsettle the symbolic and social systems that *Troilus and Criseyde* so neatly juxtaposes.

6

Coming Together: Book 2 and Pandarus

The chief framer of book 1 is Chaucer's narrator. The chief framer of book 2 is his surrogate, Pandarus, whose function within the poem closely parallels that of the narrator outside it. The two figures are linked by many devices, including the ship and the building motifs from book 1, which dominate the opening of book 2. The ship motif is attached to the narrator (after the example of Dante's *Purgatorio*, 1.1–3), who finds himself in the same "tempestous matere / Of disespeir" that engulfs Troilus (2.5–6). Pandarus feels the "shotes keene" (sharp pangs, 2.58) of love at the start of the second book, evoking the same vicarious participation in love that the narrator experienced in book 1. (Pandarus frequently repeats observations that the narrator has made earlier.) Pandarus instructs both Troilus and Criseyde in the meaning of their experiences, telling them how to act, what to say, and what to think. As he frames the action for them, he also tells the audience what to value in the text. The best measure of Pandarus's framing function is the extraordinary frequency of his various comings and goings, the numerous small moments of closure he creates on the way to the lovers' grand sexual climax of book 3. He instigates or stands at the center of most of the nearly dozen separate episodes of which book 2 consists.

The proem to book 2 focuses on the durability of language and the diversity of social customs. Because the narrator is not creating this tale (making it up) but rather reporting it, he invokes Clio, the muse of history, and his own "Muse" (2.8–9) to guide his rhyming: "Of no sentement I this endite, / But out of Latyn in my tonge it write," and again, "as myn auctour seyde" (2.13–14, 18). Although he follows his Italian model very closely, Chaucer is not translating a Latin text (he makes the same claim in 1.394); his disclaimer is deliberately misleading. He continues:

> Ye knowe ek that in forme of speche is chaunge
> Withinne a thousand yeer, and wordes tho
> That hadden pris, now wonder nyce and straunge
> Us thinketh hem, and yet thei spake hem so,
> And spedde as wel in love as men now do;
> Ek for to wynnen love in sondry ages,
> In sondry londes, sondry ben usages. (2.22–28)

Seen in the context of the history of Chaucer criticism, this elegant apology for the language and customs of ancient peoples creates irony, for both speech and customs were subsequently changed so greatly that Chaucer's came to be seen as archaic as those of Troy. That is why today it falls to specialists to defend the relevance of the past to the present and the continuity of human experience from age to age. Although some readers regard Troilus's methods in pursuing Criseyde as peculiar, the narrator does not: "For every wight which that to Rome went / Halt nat o path, or alwey o manere" (2.36–37). Arlyn Diamond notes that there are not only many ways to Rome but many Romes: that is, love itself is not universal but relative to one's time and place.[1] The approach that works for some would be ruinous to others, and one of the key issues is "opyn doyng," that is, the publicity of one's actions (2.40).

The proem to book 2 underscores the artificiality of the past, especially of social codes that come to seem quaint, even absurd. If we object to ensuing developments, we are offered a twofold rationale. We should remember, first, that the narrator is only being faithful to his source and, second, that customs differ with time and place. One of the most artificial and complicating factors in the text is the obsessive need for silence, continually used to suggest that Troilus and Criseyde, well-born figures both, are as vulnerable to public exposure as powerless commoners. The need for secrecy is a requirement of the code set forth by Andreas Capellanus:

"When made public love rarely endures."[2] This requirement forces the lovers to rely on Pandarus to arrange their meetings and authorizes him to manufacture pretenses to avoid attracting attention.

But the courtly code, as I have said earlier, does not in itself explain the obsessive need for secrecy in *Troilus and Criseyde*. Secrecy depends on a thesis about the power of speech and the power—or right—to speak. Not merely another courtly convention, secrecy redistributes power, silencing lovers and authorizing another person to act as their agent. The secret Troilus and Criseyde must keep is a secret about themselves. As a result they must, initially, allow Pandarus to represent them, even to each other. And after their affair has begun, they continue to operate according to the social structures that demand secrecy in love. The power of this secret increases as their love for each other grows; in book 3 each will say that he or she belongs wholly to the other and that love makes them one. Each will say, that is, that love makes them who they are: and this love, which constitutes their identities, cannot be known to others. Subject to love, Troilus and Criseyde are also subjects of love, subjects made by love. Because they dare not become subjects of gossip, we see how their fear of publicity makes them subjects of another sort: subjects constituted not by self-hood (as we think of individuals today) but by subjection to the social order that prescribes their behavior. This is what it means to say that they are not, as literary characters, simply independent persons (as we think of ourselves) but social beings formed and contained by the roles the social order makes available to them. The demand for secrecy obviously limits Criseyde, whose social standing is already compromised, far more than it limits Troilus, whose status as the king's son and the panderer's close friend and coconspirator is protected.

Pandarus's "grete emprise" requires that he "caste" or consult the moon (2.73–74), just as Calkas did earlier. Book 2 begins in a troubled atmosphere. Pandarus lies between sleep and wakefulness on May 3—a date important to dreamers, and the date on which Chauntecleer dreams in "The Nun's Priest's Tale."[3] Pandarus, "for al his wise speche," is so grieved by love that he, like Troilus, takes to his bed, twisting and turning (2.62). As he wakes, he hears the swallow Proigne (Procne), lamenting; the bird's song is mere "cheterynge" and "noyse" (2.68, 2.70) that wakes him. The bird's

singing evokes one of the many mythological subtexts or intertexts
that color the poem. Procne, whose story is found in Ovid's *Meta-
morphoses* (book 6), was married to Tereus, king of Thrace, who
raped Procne's sister Philomela. The sisters took revenge by feeding
Tereus the flesh of his own son and were changed into birds,
Procne into a swallow, Philomela into a nightingale.

Both birds sing in *Troilus and Criseyde*, the swallow when
Pandarus awakes, the nightingale later in this book, in a wholly
different mood, when Criseyde contemplates Troilus's love
(2.918–24). Although the nightingale's song is an admirable detail,
deftly positioned in the book, the swallow's song is one we turn
away from. She sings of a woman who avenged rape, an ugly act
that disturbs our view of what Pandarus is about to do—which is to
arrange for another man to have a woman. To say that Pandarus
plans Criseyde's rape would be gross overstatement; at the same
time, the song evokes the earlier exchange in which Pandarus has
promised to help Troilus obtain his loved one, even if she turns out
to be Pandarus's sister. A recent writer has suggested that we not
press this parallel to dark conclusions, but readers should not dismiss the ominous note that the parallel introduces.[4]

Pandarus enters Criseyde's household to find her sitting in a
courtyard with two other women hearing "a mayden" reading the
story of the siege of Thebes (found in *Thebiad* of Statius). The
reader has just finished the episode in which the soothsayer Amphiorax was swallowed into the earth. We see Criseyde within a
tightly structured, intimate social world overshadowed by the
catastrophe recounted in this ancient text: the private and the secure against the terrible, the public, and the known. She greets her
uncle warmly, saying she has dreamed of him three times the previous night and that she has taken this as a sign of good
news—presumably realized by his visit (2.90–91). Pandarus asks
her to set the tale aside, to take off her "barbe," a linen covering the
neck and chest, and join him in a dance. All these details are significant: he is asking her to unveil herself and join in the dance of
love. Criseyde responds with wit, saying that dancing is for young
wives and maidens, while she should sit "in a cave / To bidde and
rede on holy seyntes lyves," as suits a widow (2.117–19).

Pandarus skillfully promises speech—that is, news—to disrupt
Criseyde's self-imposed silence, the "stille" she returned to under

Hector's protection in book 1. News means curiosity about the larger social world that she has had to shun since her father's treason became known. Her reference to young women suggests that Criseyde, although she is indeed a widow, does not see herself as an anchoress at all; she desires to be free of social constraints. When Pandarus says that his tale is five times better than the story she is reading, her curiosity is aroused. Pandarus says he will not tell her because if she knew she would be the proudest woman in Troy. He gives her his word for this, his "borugh" or legal surety (2.134), just as he had earlier joked with Troilus about vouching for the knight's honest intentions as a would-be lover (1.1038). This tempts her further, but she feigns indifference and drops the subject, settling into easy conversation about various matters, including the war and Hector's welfare (2.153–54). Thus the great world of the Trojan War resurfaces inconspicuously in the text, a frame so completely submerged that it has become part of daily life and the subject of routine social chatter. Precisely because it is a domesticated subject, the war supplies a field of interchange between public and private.

Pandarus takes the opportunity to mention the "second" Hector, his brother Troilus ("worthi Ector the secounde," 2.158), whom Pandarus praises as a paradigm of gentilesse, truth, honor, and worthiness—the catalog of five chivalric virtues commonplace in Chaucer's age.[5] Hence Troilus, as represented by Pandarus, first appears to Criseyde within the symbolic order of idealized love, his aggression tamed, his passions subservient to his nobility. Pandarus's reply again links Hector and Troilus and confirms their virtuousness (2.171–75), and Criseyde now picks up the two names and talks briefly about the knights, noting that she has heard of Troilus's valor in battle and that he is praised by the best people (2.185–89). Pandarus specifically mentions that the previous day Troilus was "deth" to the Greeks and "sheld and lif for us" (2.201), comforting words to a widow in distress. Troilus is not only the man of the hour in battle; he has a bloody sword—as powerful an image of male domination as one can imagine—and yet he is also, Pandarus says, "the frendlieste man / Of gret estat that evere I saugh my lyve" (2.204–5). Pandarus carefully mixes aggression and tenderness here, two aspects in the knight's own character that the narrator repeatedly emphasizes in book 1.

Suddenly Pandarus says he will leave; in order to detain him, Criseyde fabricates personal business concerning "hire estat" and "hire governaunce" (2.219). Her retinue retires, acknowledging the importance of secrecy and the difficulty of obtaining it in this world. (We had quite forgotten that they were there; see 2.215–17.) This business, merely a device for leaving the two central characters alone, is quickly dropped. Exactly as he had done earlier with Troilus, Pandarus now rehearses his close acquaintance with Criseyde, saying he would never speak to upset her and that "yet were it bet my tonge for to stille / Than seye a soth that were ayeyns youre wille" (2.230–31), for she is the woman "withouten paramours" that he loves best ("withouten paramours" means "not counting lovers," not "without lovers"). She returns the compliment, and he grants her request to tell the tale he has promised (2.251–52).

Pandarus decides to keep his account short and simple so as not to alarm her—the narrator shows us his thinking process, in which he calculates the effect of speech—but in fact his account is a very long speech replete with the proverbial wisdom for which Pandarus is famous (2.315–85). He begins with a warning not to waste good opportunities; although everyone is, at some time, destined for good fortune, if they turn it aside they have only themselves to blame (2.284–85). He assures her that he has only her best intentions at heart (2.295–301) and tries to calm her mounting fears, manifest in her changing color and fearful shaking.

She urges him to get to the point. He does: "The noble Troilus, so loveth the. / That, but ye helpe, it wol his bane be" (2.319–20). If she refuses Troilus, Pandarus himself will cut his own throat (2.324–26). In fact, Pandarus says, Troilus is already among the walking dead ("I se hym dyen, ther he goth upryght," 2.333) and, distraught, seeks his death—all this because of Criseyde's beauty. "Wo worth that beaute that is routheles," he warns: woe unto beauty that has no compassion (2.346). Her refusal will cause two deaths, Troilus's and his own. And he would rather that all three of them died, Pandarus concludes, than he (Pandarus) "sholde ben his [Troilus's] baude" (2.353)—"baude" being the precise name for the role Pandarus plays.

Pandarus asks only that Criseyde show favor to Troilus, not that she bind herself to him (2.358–60), and if she simply does that much, she will have saved Troilus's life along with his own. Pandarus anticipates her objections, saying that the worst she could fear is that others would see Troilus visit her: he wisely raises her gravest objection, which is public rather than personal, showing us that her own feelings about love are secondary and that appearances govern all. Emphasizing a nonsexual type of love, Pandarus tells his niece that only a fool would fail to see that these visits are only the "love of frendshipe" (2.371). And because Troilus is careful, and meets with praise everywhere he goes (as they have just said), "What fors were it though al the town byhelde?" Indeed, in Troy "love of frendes" rules (2.378–79). Pandarus's emphasis on public knowledge of the affair returns us to the scales on which Troilus and Criseyde weigh their actions as they calculate the dangers of speech and silence. Here we glimpse Criseyde's private thoughts: "I shal felen what he meneth, ywis," she says (2.387)—an intrusion that reminds us that Pandarus is not in control of the narrative after all and that the narrator has an interest in Criseyde's secret as well as spoken responses. Criseyde asks what Pandarus would have her do, and he replies that she should reward love with love; he reminds her that she is not getting any younger and that age humbles proud women.

Criseyde weeps, wishes she were dead, and blames the world for her predicament (2.410). How can one who claims to be her best friend advise her to enter into an affair? Indeed, she says, had she herself initiated an affair with Achilles, or Troilus, or Hector, she would have been reproached by Pandarus and everyone else (2.415–20). She cannot believe that this story is the "paynted proces" Pandarus has promised (2.424). She calls on Pallas for help (2.426). Pandarus appears to be deeply offended, saying that she obviously regards his death—and Troilus's—very lightly. He swears on the gods that he meant no harm (2.435–38) and pretends to storm out. "The ferfulleste wight / That myghte be," she detains him when she realizes that Pandarus is earnest. She begins to calculate (2.450–57). If he dies in her presence (he has a knife, we know), "it wol be no solas," she thinks (2.460); hence she must be careful: "It nedeth me ful sleighly for to pleie" (2.462). Although her estate "lith in a jupartie," she agrees to save both her uncle's life and Troilus's (2.465–69). She will take the lesser of two evils and limit her consent to "good chere," the least Pandarus has asked for (2.470–71).

She thus enters into the bargaining that soon brings her to Troilus's bed.

Pandarus has won Criseyde over by appealing to courtliness and demonstrating his skill in manipulating public opinion. But his extended and cautious proposal, even with its posturing, acknowledges her power, which is fully displayed in her response, which is brief but no less calculating and assured than his presentation. Her performance is especially impressive because Criseyde, unlike Pandarus, has not had time to rehearse. She does what she must rather than what she wishes to do, for she cannot love a man against her will. Even if both Troilus and Pandarus die as a result, and all the world "on o day be my fo" (2.488), she vows to do no more. Here Criseyde asserts in speech an independence regarding public opinion in a way that she will never assert in deed. Here we see her power to resist the forces that seek to shape—that is, to frame, construct, and confine—her character and her will.

Pandarus claims to be satisfied and confirms her agreement. With their bargain complete, they turn to other matters until Criseyde asks Pandarus how he learned about Troilus's love for her and if anybody else knows about it (the latter, we can assume, is as much on her mind as the former; 2.500–502). Pandarus lies, saying that they met in a garden by a well, discussed the siege of the city, played games, and slept. In his sleep Troilus spoke to the god of love, repenting his heresies against love. Pandarus learned no more until a few days later—and here his tale encounters truth for the first time—when he came upon Troilus lamenting in his room. Pandarus demonstrates his ample abilities to weave fictions in his construction of the lover's encounter with the god of love by a well in a garden, a scene with many analogues in medieval French romance.[6] But when he says, "Ye woot that myn entent is cleene" (2.580), we can all believe him, for he has accomplished exactly and only what he promised Troilus he would do; any false stories have merely enhanced the facts.

Pandarus introduces a sexual subtext into the ensuing discussion that both speakers recognize and seem to enjoy. When he tells Criseyde that "wel in the ryng than is the ruby set," he means on the surface that the lovers are well matched; but when he adds, "Whan ye ben his al hool as he is youre," the sexual act implicit in putting a gem into its setting appears to surface, as her embar-

rassment—"Nay, therof spak I nought, ha, ha!"—seems to acknowledge (2.585–89). They conclude their discussion, agreeing that
there is no offense, and Criseyde, alone for the first time, is eager to
inspect her thoughts. She retires to her "closet," or private compartment, a new frame for her:

> And set hire doun as stylle as any ston,
> And every word gan up and down to wynde
> That he had seyd, as it com hire to mynde. (2.600–602)

She finds no reason to be afraid, for even though a man is so
in love with a woman that his heart breaks, she does not have to
return that love "but if hire leste" (2.609). The reader does well to
contrast Criseyde's cool appraisal, which concludes with the realization that she is only as bound as she wishes to be, with Troilus's
meditation on the image of her fixed in his heart (1.297–98). Both
are alone in their most private places, concentrating on the affair
that lies before them; she weighs her options while he writhes in
pain. Troilus has created the text; she analyzes it.

Her meditation is interrupted by a public outcry at the return
of Troilus from the battlefield, the first of the hero's two appearances outside her window in book 2. (The second is staged by Pandarus within his construction of the romance.) The first now un-
folds, an apparently coincidental event engineered by the narrator,
whose framing action Pandarus emulates in this detail as in so
many others. Troilus and his retinue are returning from a successful fight; his horse is wounded and so the hero rides slowly.
The narrator describes the scene in loving detail: Troilus is "fulfilled
of heigh prowesse, / For bothe he hadde a body and a myght / To
don that thing, as well as hardynesse" (2.632–34). Helmet shat-
tered, shield scarred with blows and arrows, Troilus is hailed by the
people as their "joye," the "holder up of Troye" (2.643–44). Troilus
handles the outcry with becoming modesty, keeping his eyes low.
Beholding the scene from her window, Criseyde is nearly over-
come—"Who yaf me drynke?" she asks herself (2.651), and then
considers that this is the man who will die unless she grants him
her love (2.654–55). She enumerates his attributes, finding that
"moost hire favour was, for his distresse / Was al for hire"
(2.663–64).

Criseyde persuades herself that the proposed affair has many attractions. As her resistance wears down, the narrator intervenes to defend the seeming suddenness of her change of heart. He reminds us that she is not giving Troilus her love but only that she "gan enclyne / To like hym first," and that Troilus earns her love "by proces and by good servyse"—in other words, only after the necessary courtly rituals (2.674–75, 2.678). This emphasis on construction in Criseyde's deliberations emerges in succeeding stanzas. If her uncle will not cease to press Troilus's case, she must decide what she will do. It would be honorable to deal with one so noble; it would both advance her position (her "estat") and heal his woe (2.706–7). Indeed, since he is a king's son, it would be dangerous to her position to scorn him.

This convenient transition from opportunity to obligation shows how she rationalizes compromise (2.712). There is measure in all things—that is, there is a calculated, mediated compromise always available—and a proverb reinforces her point: one can forbid drunkenness (that is, excess) but not drinking (for it is natural). Criseyde reminds herself that she has long known of Troilus's virtues; he is no braggart and, in any case, she will never be his so completely—"I nyl hym nevere so cherice" (2.726)—that he will be able to boast about her or use "swich a clause" to bind her (2.728). Her self-possession becomes increasingly clear: she cannot help it if he loves her, and if people discover that he does, she remains blameless (2.730–32). In Troy Troilus is second only to Hector; he could have any woman he wants, but he has chosen her, indeed "oon the faireste, out of drede, / And goodlieste" in the city (2.746–47). Her conclusion is a famous assertion:

> I am myn owene womman, wel at ese—
> I thank it God—as after myn estat,
> Right yong, and stonde unteyd in lusty leese,
> Withouten jalousie or swich debat:
> Shal noon housbonde seyn to me "Chek mat!" (2.750–54)

Hence she resolves to have him without shame to herself; but no sooner has she made this resolution than its darker aspects appear to her. A dark thought "gan thorugh hire soule pace" as if it were a cloud passing over the sun, the narrator says (2.768). She becomes frightened at the thought of giving up her liberty

(2.771–75). Then, in a demonstration of how Chaucer orchestrates the speech of characters with that of the narrator, so that the independence of their observations—and personalities—is sometimes doubtful, Criseyde uses the cloud figure herself: "For evere som mystrust or nice strif/Ther is in love, som cloude is over that sonne" (2.780–81).

The following stanzas formulate and restate Criseyde's pessimistic views of love and the danger that love poses to her reputation. A counterreading of the poem's symbolic order of courtly love, they reframe that order from her point of view. In a consciously formed philosophy of gender, she states that women do not know about the complications of love but weep; their misfortune is their "owen wo to drynke" (2.784). Tongues wag and men are faithless; when their desire is satisfied, their love is over; but the harm to the women's reputations endures. Women have often been betrayed by a pointless kind of love that begins in nothing and ends there: "That erst was nothing, into nought it torneth" (2.798). If she enters into love, she will have to please many besides Troilus; she will have to placate the public to keep them from speaking ill of her (2.800–805). Yet this sharply negative prospect finally emerges as a challenge, and tossing off another bit of proverbial wisdom— nothing ventured, nothing gained (2.807–8)—she goes out "to pleye" (2.812).

The long section just concluded (2.701–812) is literally framed between window scenes, two idealized views of Troilus as hero. Criseyde goes into the garden with her three nieces—Flexippe, Tharbe, and Antigone, the three with whom she was listening to the maiden reading when Pandarus arrived—and a group of others. Antigone sings a love song that answers, systematically if unconsciously, the doubts about love that Criseyde has just enumerated for herself, filtering Criseyde's thoughts through the consciousness of a lyric created by the narrator, just as Troilus's song in book 1 introduced the perspective of a new genre to illuminate his thoughts and recast them.[7] In effect, Antigone's song reasserts the symbolic order that Criseyde's meditation has questioned. In book 2 commentary comes from an outside source: it is one of several such influences and stimuli that create the impression that, self-possessed though she is, she requires external pressures—that is, pressures from the social world—before she can decide. The song thanks the god of love for leading the singer out of fear into joy and security (2.831–33); her lover is devoted and without danger, a "welle of worthynesse, / Of trouthe grownd, mirour of goodlihed" (2.838–39, 2.841–42). The life of love is "the righte life," where in "alle manere vice and synne" are banished (2.851–52). Love is none the worse because some defame it, just as the sun is none the worse because men's feeble eyes try to behold it; this particular image answers Criseyde's belief that it is no dishonor to the lady if a man loves her (2.731–32; here 2.862–63). Antigone's song concludes with an image of exchanged hearts: she will love her knight, in whom "myn herte growen is so faste, / And his in me, that it shal evere laste" (2.872–73). This image soon reappears in Criseyde's dream. Having carefully printed the song "in hire herte faste" (2.900), she takes leave of her retinue and retires to bed.

Near her chamber wall a nightingale sings "in his briddes wise a lay / Of love" (2.921–22) as Criseyde falls into a deep sleep. In her dream, an eagle descends, inserts his claws under her breast, "and out hire herte he rente, and that anon, / And dide his herte into hire brest to gon." Faced with this startling apparition she feels neither pain nor fear, and the eagle flies away "with herte left for herte" (2.925–31). She is left in silence, and the significance of her dream, which prefigures and overlays much of the succeeding action, is never discussed. The silence preserves her isolation and privacy; no interpretation—no reading by another—follows. The dream remains her secret, a moment interiorized and kept from others; if it has any influence on her subsequent behavior, that is not discussed. Chaucer's readers, however, greatly impressed by the vision, have not hesitated to offer a variety of views about its significance.[8] But the reader now knows all that is necessary to explain her conduct during the affair that is about to commence: her habit of deliberation, a slightly evasive quality that shifts responsibility from her to her circumstances, a desire both to preserve her independence and to be protected, even overpowered, in love.

Here, at the midpoint of the book, the narrator returns to Troilus, who awaits news of Pandarus's visit to Criseyde. Pandarus now reproduces his manipulation of Criseyde in his managing of Troilus. He rouses the prostrate hero with jokes and dines with him. Then, when the knight's retinue is dismissed, they retire (2.948–49). Eager for details, Troilus presses Pandarus, who lightheartedly asks to be left alone and then adds that Criseyde has been persuaded to consent to the affair: "Hire love of frendshipe have I to the wonne, / And therto hath she leyd hire feyth to borwe" (2.962–63). As if being reborn, Troilus revives and thanks Venus. In language that as a happy lover he flatly contradicts in book 3, he claims that he has been cured and freed—"al brosten ben my bondes" (2.976). Later, in his Boethian reinterpretation of this image, he hails the power of love to create bonds, not loose them. He now asks Pandarus what to do next, and Pandarus suggests that Troilus write a letter to beseech Criseyde's mercy (2.1006–1008). He also tells Troilus to ride before her window, "right in thi beste gere," salute her, and, above all, keep his composure (2.1012–20).

The letter, as Pandarus describes it, is to be a masterpiece of feigned—indeed, framed—sentiment, "biblotte[d]" with the hero's tears, not stating matters in overly complex or "scryvenyssh" ways, not belaboring the point (2.1026–29). He promises to bring her answer himself. Heartened, Troilus writes about his love, apologizing for faults in his style and attributing them to his devotion to her. His sentiment is not artificial; when be bathes his signet ring in his "salte teris" and kisses the letter before sending it on its way, there is little room to doubt his sincerity (2.1086–92). When Pandarus delivers the letter the next day, Criseyde greets him as if he is a ship blown into port and asks, "How ferforth be ye put in loves daunce?" (2.1106), as if the affair were his rather than hers.

Pandarus dissimulates his reason for coming, saying there is a Greek spy in town who tells "newe thinges" and makes it necessary for him to speak to her privately (2.1112). This indirect and utterly gratuitous reference to the war seems designed to menace his niece as well as to ensure some privacy for the ensuing discussion. She refuses to read the letter and asks that Pandarus return it; her puzzling hesitation registers her fear of the affair, as Pandarus's response suggests: he protests that he would rather be struck dead than bring her a dangerous letter (2.1147–48). He thrusts the letter into her bosom, challenging her to pluck it out so that people will stare at them. "I kan abyde til they be gon," she replies, with a smile, and says that he should compose the reply because she will not (2.1158–61). Pandarus, fully in charge of the affair, thus superintends both the letter, the artifact, and the framework within which Criseyde responds to what Troilus has written. The tension disappears as they go off to dinner, laughing merrily. Before they dine, however, she calls her women to her and retreats into her chamber (2.1172–76).

Her appraisal of Troilus's letter is swift and positive; she recognizes a good style and puts the letter away. On the way to dinner she surprises Pandarus and catches him by his hood, trapping him in a joking way that suggests a role reversal (i.e., his trapping her) and that plays on the binding imagery that we find throughout the text. After dinner Pandarus continues to direct his script, bringing Criseyde to the window to discuss her reply to the letter. He volunteers to write it, but she says she knows how, although she doesn't know what to say (2.1205). She withdraws into a "closet" or private compartment, claiming that "this is the firste lettre / That evere I wroot, ye, al or any del" (2.1213–14). She unfetters her heart a bit, thanks Troilus for his pains, and asserts her independence: she will be like a sister to him and hopes that will be enough for him (2.1223–24). When she returns to Pandarus, she claims to have been constrained to write and that she never did anything "with more peyne / Than writen this" (2.1231–32). Pandarus is actually happy to hear this, for, to quote a proverb, "Impressiounes lighte / Ful lightly ben ay redy to the flighte"; it has been hard to "grave" or make an impression on her heart, but at last he has done so (2.1238–41).

When Troilus suddenly appears with a small retinue, Pandarus calls Criseyde to the window for a scene that, as if in imitation of the narrator, he has elaborately staged for her benefit. Troilus salutes her, so overwhelmed that he is barely able to stay on his horse. Criseyde appraises his appearance and is deeply impressed with "his persoun, his aray, his look, his chere" (2.1267). The narrator crassly wishes that Criseyde, resistant up to now, be firmly pierced with a thorn—an image of penetration (2.1272–74) whose suppressed sexual content connects to the next image. Pandarus, finding that "the iron is hot" (2.1276), urges her to consent to Troilus, but she resists: she will reward him with a glimpse only (2.1295). Pandarus thinks to himself that her resistance cannot last more than two years (long enough, of course, but perhaps a widow's waiting period) and withdraws when it is evening to visit Troilus.

He finds Troilus in bed and in despair, but rouses him with the letter Criseyde has sent (2.1314–16). Her letter balances encouragement and resistance, but Troilus makes his own interpretation and decides that it is "al for the beste" that she wrote (2.1324). Her words are veiled "under shield" (2.1327) and are difficult to gauge, but he allows his hopes to grow, for just as an oak comes from a small seed, great desire comes from the letter (2.1335–37).

During the following interval, Troilus keeps his passions stirred with Pandarus's assistance, allowing them to grow, nurturing them, but also seeing his fate as a lover in terms of luck, as if casting dice for a favorable outcome, another instance of divination (2.1347). Pandarus urges Troilus to leave things to his shaping powers, which have been invoked repeatedly (2.1359–65). He promises that Troilus will find reward in two days (not the two years he thought about when last with Criseyde) and suggests that what the lover needs—he has good authority for this—is a secret place in which to reveal his love and make a good impression when the lady hears and sees "the giltlees in distresse" (2.1371–72). He should understand that although natural inclination (personified as "Kynde") may urge Criseyde to pity the lover, "Danger" (another personification, possibly taken from *The Romance of the Rose*)[9] keeps her distant and wary.

Pandarus likens her assent to felling a tree: a massive oak falls with a single blow only after many people have hacked at it. It takes great effort to fell such a tree, but once down it stays down; a slender reed that bends with every breeze returns to its position easily (2.1380–90). Winning Criseyde is like felling the oak: it is a "gret empryse," an echo of language used earlier (2.73) to describe Pandarus's orchestration of the affair, and, though the task requires much patience, it brings lasting rewards. It is also a disturbing image of conquest and death, although its grim connotations are, characteristically, left undeveloped.

Using images of life and death—the small seed and the felled tree—Pandarus has analyzed the two forces influencing Criseyde: her natural inclination as a woman, and her sense of self-preservation and caution. He advances his "empryse" by arranging to use society, the lovers' enemy, on their behalf. This court scene links book 2 to the next book and shows Pandarus's framing activity at its most ambitious and deceitful. Pandarus enlists Deiphebus,

Troilus's favorite brother, in an elaborate scheme that easily deceives the entire royal household as well as Criseyde. Pandarus reports to Deiphebus that some citizens are speaking against his niece; they "wolden don oppressioun, / And wrongfully han hire possessioun" (2.1418–19). Deiphebus immediately agrees to be her champion and asks how he may help. Pandarus suggests that he invite Criseyde to come to him to make her complaint, saying that her enemies will hear of it and become frightened (2.1435). Moreover, Pandarus suggests, it would be well to have some others on hand to strengthen the impression of unity on her behalf. Deiphebus agrees to ask Helen, Paris, Hector, and Troilus to take part (2.1447–58). Pandarus demonstrates how easily rumor passes as fact and—worse still—how, in a world ruled by silence and secrecy, the most influential people can be led astray by a single, industrious figure.

Pandarus's next step is to frighten Criseyde into seeking Deiphebus's assistance, which he does by manufacturing a story about "false Poliphete," who is supposedly bringing "advocacies newe" against her (2.1467–69). This story confirms Criseyde's view of the world as a menacing place, although she notes that if Poliphete were not befriended by Aeneas and Antenor "in swich manere cas" she would pay no attention to his plots (2.1473–74). She understands Antenor, Aeneas, and Poliphete to be united against her, and although we have no way of knowing what there is to sustain her impression, it is nonetheless clear that Criseyde has a clear view of the political and social worlds in which she moves. She has no desire to fight her detractors; if they take everything, she will still have "ynough" (2.1477–78). Pandarus assures her that there will be no struggle, for he has obtained from Deiphebus a promise to protect her, and others are supporting her. As they discuss the case, Deiphebus himself arrives to invite her to dinner, and Criseyde accepts.

Pandarus then visits Troilus and persuades him to take part in a feigned illness that nicely and ironically underscores the hero's real sickness in love. This, Pandarus promises, is an opportunity. "Somtyme a man mot telle his owen peyne," he says: "Bileve it, and she shal han on the routhe" (2.1501–1502). Pandarus is perfectly candid about his "blending" of Deiphebus (2.1496) and the "sleyghte" he will use to conceal Troilus's condition (2.1512).

Troilus will go to Deiphebus, pretend to be sick, and take to his bed—and indeed, since "sik is he that is in sorwe" (2.1523), Troilus need not find this difficult. The hero agrees that he needs no prompting to pretend illness, "for I am sik in ernest, douteles, / So that wel neigh I sterve for the peyne" (2.1529-30). Invoking another menacing hunting metaphor, Pandarus advises Troilus to wait at the meeting point. Pandarus will drive "the deer unto thi bowe." This explicit sexual language prompts no response in the text in the form of a reaction from either Troilus or the narrator (2.1534-35).

Troilus does as told: he visits his brother's house, says he is sick, and is put to bed, but not before he says that he too will assist Criseyde (2.1549-50). Everyone gathers for dinner, including Criseyde and Pandarus, but only God and Pandarus know what is to happen, the narrator says, thereby linking these two makers or shapers (2.1561). When they hear that Troilus is ill, they all have various proposals for curing him; Criseyde says nothing but knows that "best koud I yet ben his leche" (2.1582). A testimony in praise of Troilus follows. Criseyde absorbs it; her face is sober, but her heart laughs (2.1592). The subject turns to Criseyde, and Pandarus repeats his lies about the plot against her: "He rong hem out a pro-ces lik a belle / Upon hire foo," the narrator says (2.1615-16), and everyone denounces Poliphete. When Helen asks if Hector or Troilus know about this, Pandarus replies that they do, but since Troilus is in the house, Criseyde herself should speak to him (2.1629-30), thus assuring the private meeting that Pandarus promised Troilus the previous day.

Pandarus rushes in to tell Troilus that Criseyde is coming; but since only a few can be allowed in the room at once, only Helen and Deiphebus enter. Helen asks Pandarus to explain the situation to Troilus, a moment of high comedy, of course, since Troilus is fully advised of the trumped-up nature of the charges. Troilus's part in the ruse now surfaces: he has "a tretys and a lettre" from Hector, he says (2.1697), and he would like to ask Helen and Deiphebus about it. They leave to ponder the letter; Pandarus tells Criseyde that Helen and the two men wish to see her and suggests that she bring Antigone with her. Then, at the last minute, Criseyde's niece is left behind ("The lesse prees, the bet," Pandarus says [2.1718]), and Criseyde and Pandarus enter alone. Pandarus urges Criseyde to be gentle with Troilus, to remember "which oon he is, / And in what plit he lith" (2.1737–38) and to waste no time ("while folk is blent, lo, al the tyme is wonne," 2.1743). Before they enter, the narrator takes us to the point at which book 3 begins, with Troilus wondering what he will say now that he finally "shulde hire preye / Of love" (2.1756–57).

Pandarus dominates book 2, fabricating threats to Criseyde, exploiting the reputation of influential men (Poliphete, who is at least a friend to the powerful), and urging both Troilus and Criseyde to enter into adventures that neither is inclined to initiate on his or her own: Criseyde because she is wary, Troilus because he is unable to negotiate love on his own. Pandarus poses a real threat to Criseyde, whom he manipulates on two accounts—her fear of the Greeks and her fear of the loss of her reputation. These fears exist at the intersection of her public and private persons—her life as the daughter of a traitor and her life as the beloved of one of the city's finest warriors. Her public vulnerability, her weak position in the Trojan political structure, is exploited to rob her of power (at least, of self-possession) in terms of the private relationship being structured for her, around her, by both Troilus and Pandarus. The court scene with which book 2 concludes concentrates our attention on the interplay of public and private issues, on the intersection of speech and silence, in the narrative.

7

7

Falling in Place:
Book 3 and Boethius

The idea of the frame that has been pursued on the level of narrative in book 1 and on the level of character in book 2 functions on a larger scale in the remainder of the poem. The frames of the narrator and Pandarus are easily identified and easily rationalized; the investments of both figures in the story are obvious. The narrator's framing is unremittingly self-conscious; Pandarus's framing is betrayed by his interest in the affair between Troilus and Criseyde, an interest that is more material than ethereal. Both lovers rely on him to shape events. The narrator and Pandarus share a thesis that unites the first two books: romantic love cannot succeed without the intervention and the moderating influence of intermediaries. The narrator insists that love stories in the past must be translated for contemporary audiences. Pandarus demonstrates both that love affairs in courtly societies must be mediated by go-betweens who protect the secrecy and thus ensure the safety of the lovers, and that the go-between may have his own motives in promoting the affair. While love stories need a sympathetic narrator who does not criticize lovers, love affairs demand subterfuge. Love, it seems, must be framed by interests outside the lovers' exclusive circle, controlled by forces that can contain love and ensure that it does not threaten social order. The framers of book 1 and book 2 reveal their interests in the story through the frames they supply for it. The narrator and Pandarus continue to steer events, but the

82

framers most important to the remaining books are abstract forces, ideas and ideologies that maintain social systems in ways less detectable than those of the narrator and the go-between.

The major framing force of book 3 is love itself, and the accompanying thesis is that love creates universal harmony by controlling all creation, by compelling nature, nations, lovers, and friends to live in peaceful coexistence. The ideal is derived from *The Consolation of Philosophy*, which supplies the ultimate source for the proem to book 3. Lady Philosophy says:

> All this harmonious order of things is achieved by love which rules the earth and the seas, and commands the heavens. But if love should slack the reins, all that is now joined in mutual love would wage continual war, and strive to tear apart the world which is now sustained in friendly concord by beautiful motion. Love binds together people joined by a sacred bond; love binds sacred marriages by chaste affections; love makes the laws which join true friends. (Boethius, book 2, poem 8)

Love is a *binding* force. An ideal far beyond the reach of fiction, love furnishes a code of conduct that binds all the characters. For Troilus and Criseyde, love is both more and less. At first it is a discourse of human passion that brings them together for an extended period of sexual and psychological happiness in which they achieve nearly perfect parity. But the private order of this love is easily superseded by other orders, in particular the public order that binds citizens to their state. In a world torn apart by war, as Troy is, "friendly concord" between lovers must be sacrificed to other loyalties. In book 4 the concord between Troilus and Criseyde is interrupted; in book 5 it is the first of the poem's social harmonies to be destroyed. Book 3 presents Chaucer's view of how the ideal of universal love, a glorious symbolic system and grandest narrative frame of the poem, controls violence, creates peace and harmony, and ensures that the elements retain their proper place in the cosmos.

The Boethian vision of love binds social and natural elements together into a coherent whole. The proem to book 3, which translates this vision into images belonging to the chief symbolic systems of the poem, celebrates the power of Venus to tame Mars. Thus the system of courtly love reaches to the gods: the narrator praises the female deity's power to calm the violent male. So broad a vision defines the place of each character and assigns moral value to each character's words and actions. Filtered through the consciousness of Troilus in particular, the thesis that love compels order is either perverted or at least partially misunderstood. But the proem supplies the thesis in purer form, although still framed by the narrator. For a time, both Criseyde and Troilus share in this symbolic system and believe in it; as they do so, they achieve something like real parity as lovers, a moment of aesthetic and artistic success the poem never betters. Elizabeth Salter has praised Chaucer's vision in book 3 as a description of love that admits "its dignity as well as its vulnerability" and that gives "serious status to bodily as well as spiritual compassion." This vision, she believes, reaches the limits of his artistic and moral responsibility; in the following books "the admirable recklessness of his actions has to be paid for."[1]

Book 3 moves to the lovers' sustained bliss in three parts: the concluding scene in the house of Deiphebus arranged in book 2 and a subsequent discussion between Pandarus and Troilus (3.50–3.420); a long central episode in which Pandarus brings the lovers to his house for their first night together (to 3.1555); and a two-part conclusion in which Pandarus "debriefs" the lovers. The book closes with Troilus himself quoting the Boethian praise of love quoted in the proem and thus internalizing the frame of this book.

The invocation to Venus in the proem not only acclaims the universal healing powers of love but specifically attributes both human worth and happiness to love. Love constitutes a "law of kynde" or a natural inclination for gods and humans alike that creates not only personal friendship but also political harmony. "Ye holden regne and hous in unitee," the narrator writes; "ye sothfast cause of frendship ben also" (3.29–30). Thus, although Venus alone knows why certain people love each other, why "this fissh, and naught that," is caught in love's trap (3.35–36), her powers are far greater. Venus creates harmony on a vast scale; she has created a universal "lawe" that no one can easily resist; love is a compulsion, an ordering force, that extends from the most intimate to the most public domains. Yet we remember that, at the start of book 2, the narrator quotes the proverb claiming that, in matters of love, "ecch contree hath his lawes" (2.42). That is, even though public roles demand conformity, individual identity follows dictates of its own.

Thus the citizen who is constituted by public discourse stands in conflict with the person possessing secrets that he or she must keep.

Just as the narrator ponders his writing problem, Troilus too, at the opening of the book, rehearses the speech he will deliver when Criseyde appears in his room. Troilus struggles to master the personal code that tells lovers how to act and what to say. "That word is good," he decides, "and this shal be my cheere; / This nyl I nought foryeten in no wise" (3.54–55). But when Pandarus leads Criseyde into the room, the hero's composure is short-lived. Criseyde announces herself and says that she comes only to thank him and to ask of his "lordshipe eke / Continuance" (3.76–77). Troilus is too embarrassed to reply; he knows that her alarm is the result of Pandarus's lies on his behalf. Troilus blushes deeply and his mind goes blank: his carefully rehearsed speech "is thorugh his wit ironne" (3.84). His confusion is not lost on her, "for she was wis, and loved hym nevere the lasse" (3.86).

The skills of the lovers are neatly juxtaposed: his bumbling performance is noted and excused by his cool yet sympathetic mistress. It appears that both are acting now, playing their parts, although she commands her role with infinitely greater skills. When speech returns, he can say only, "Mercy, mercy, swete herte!" (3.98). But then he manages to declare his devotion and to praise her. Pandarus, his tears flowing, nudges his niece and asks that she either "make of this thing an ende, / Or sle us both at ones er ye wende" (3.118–19). She tells Pandarus that Troilus should tell her "the fyn of his entente," for "yet wist I nevere wel what that he mente" (3.125–26). Her request is practical, polite, and wholly reasonable. For if she has heard many words about him, she has also heard only a few words from him. Troilus desires that she look on him kindly and accept his services "[w]ithouten braunche of vice on any wise," so that he will be able to serve her always (3.127–47). How can she refuse? Pandarus asks. She first replies to Pandarus, not to her lover, asking that Troilus respect her honor "with wit and bisynesse" (3.165). When she turns to Troilus her tone changes:

"But natheles, this warne I yow," quod she,
"A kynges sone although ye be, ywys,
Ye shal namore han sovereignete
Of me in love, than right in that cas is;

85

N'y nyl forbere, if that ye don amys,
To wratthe yow; and whil that ye me serve,
Chericen yow right after ye disserve." (3.169–75)

As she takes Troilus in her arms, Pandarus falls to his knees to thank Cupid and Venus. He suddenly remembers that Helen and Deiphebus will soon return to interrupt this meeting and suggests that the lovers meet at his house. There, he says to them, he can "shape youre comynge; / And eseth there youre hertes right ynough." A brief laugh acknowledges the sexual implications of his offer (3.196–99). Before the others return, Criseyde leaves.

It is now time for Pandarus to process the guilt that follows his success. This he does in a long speech in which the dimensions of private and public social worlds are more clearly sketched than anywhere else in the work. Pandarus states that he has done his part "to brynge [Troilus] to joye out of distresse" (3.245) and that this is more than he will do again for anyone, even his own brother (3.251). He has become

Bitwixen game and ernest, swich a meene
As maken wommen unto men to comen;
Al sey I nought, thow wost wel what I meene. (3.254–56)

He acknowledges his pandering role but claims that he has not arranged this affair "for coveitise" but rather only to ease Troilus's misery. Troilus must "kep hire out of blame" and "save alwey hire name" (3.265–66). Such a speech hardly absolves Pandarus from moral responsibility, but it registers his awareness that the gap between the safety of privacy and the risk of publicity has been bridged and that Criseyde's reputation is now in danger.

Pandarus worries that "she is my nece deere, / And I hire em, and traitour eke yfeere!" (3.273–74). He thus reinforces the paradigm of the betraying father figure reminiscent of Criseyde's relationship with Calkas; but there is more in the word, for "traitour" here comes from the Italian *trattator*, or procurer.[2] Since he has served as a panderer or go-between, his concern for his own reputation is well founded, for he could be accused of "the werste trecherie" ever (3.278)—treason, but not to the state. In order to protect their mutual vulnerability and see to it that Troilus "us nevere wreye" (betray; 3.284), he cautions Troilus to hold his tongue (that is, not boast of his affair) and curb "diffusioun of speche," or indiscretions. He stresses the importance of holding in "secree" a woman's love and cannot find the name—Panderer, his own—for those who violate that confidence (3.312–20). This long speech discloses the full nature of Pandarus's role, now stripped of the jocular enthusiasm that has hitherto characterized it. Pandarus unframes his joviality; in its place he installs a sober frame whose serious language emphasizes the dangers of the affair that is about to begin.

The narrator renews the illness metaphor with Criseyde as physician, a metaphor that emerged in the previous book (2.1582) when she allegorized herself as a physician ("leche") who could heal Troilus of his malady (3.119, 3.168). Now cured, Troilus seems to bloom like a wood or a hedge in spring. He dates his first sight of Criseyde to April (3.360), which, amid other suggestions of spring-time regeneration, invokes "The General Prologue" to *The Canterbury Tales*. In his earnest reply, Troilus assures Pandarus that the secret will be kept (3.369–71); he declares that he would rather be killed by Achilles (who does in fact kill him) or be the prisoner of Agamemnon (who is leading the siege of Troy) than reveal the secret (3.380–85). He understands that what Pandarus has done was undertaken "for compaignie" (3.396), for companionship; it was not "a bauderye" but "gentilesse, / Compassioun, and felawship, and trist" (3.402–403).

Amplifying his efforts to ease Pandarus's conscience, Troilus demonstrates how words can change the perception of a morally ambiguous act; as he puts it, "Departe it so, for wyde-wher is wist / How that ther is diversite requered / Bytwixen thynges like, as I have lered" (3.404–6).[3] That is, everywhere it is necessary to distinguish between the words used to describe similar actions. Eager to show Pandarus that he approves, Troilus continues:

> And that thow knowe I thynke nought ne wene
> That this servise a shame be or jape,
> I have my faire suster Polixene,
> Cassandre, Eleyne, or any of the frape—
> Be she nevere so fair or wel yshape,
> Tel me which thow wilt of everychone,
> To han for thyn, and lat me thanne allone. (3.407–13)

That is, if Pandarus will simply tell Troilus which one of his sisters he would like to have (which one of the "frape," meaning "company or multitude" but also "rabble"), Troilus will arrange it. Commenting on this ugly offer, Carolyn Dinshaw writes, "No critic, to my knowledge, has been able to make adequate sense of this moment when the larger social reality of Troy erupts in the narrative, suddenly impinges upon the private world to which the narrative has heretofore been devoted." As she notes, we see Troilus participating in two moral realms, the private, in which he values Criseyde above all else, and the public, in which women exist to be exchanged by men.[4] But we should recall that, in book 1, Pandarus promised that he would obtain the woman who caused Troilus's sorrow, even if she were Pandarus's sister (1.861). Pandarus's references to his procuring activities degraded both men in book 1; Troilus here doubles the fault. The eruption of the social has not, therefore, taken place only here. Nor does the public ("larger social reality") impinge on the private world in this episode, I would say, so much as disclose how the public continuously constitutes the private, how the social role creates the individual's ongoing sense of self. Dinshaw writes that the "view of women as gifts, as tokens of exchange, is more basic to the relations of men in Troy than is the view of women as singular and unique" (61). Troilus's offer not only underscores the system used to value women but even more plainly reveals the homosocial bond between Troilus and Pandarus. The singularity and uniqueness of the men should not be inferred from their denial of these qualities to Criseyde; we cannot suppose that they function on a different level or are realized as individual when she is not. These characters occupy different places in the symbolic and social systems of the poem (they are not, obviously, equally powerful), but they are all subject to the logic of the same system and subjects of the same system.

Thus the hero's attempt to clarify the ambiguity of what Pandarus has done ends by confirming it. Their common interests (and moral equivalence) now demonstrated, Troilus urges Pandarus to continue his "gret empryse"—a collocation used by the narrator at the start and by Pandarus at the end of book 2 (2.73, 2.1391, 3.416).

Troilus's deeds prove as good as his words. The narrator describes how in the days that followed he guarded his secret closely, kept "from every wight as fer as is the cloude" (3.433), and carried on a career of exceptional valor "in Martes heigh servyse." He honors both his public role, fighting on the battlefield by day, and his interior, private sense of self, lying awake by night, contemplating his "service" to Criseyde (3.437–41). Both roles are constituted by social expectations. During this time he sees Criseyde but they handle themselves with circumspection "in this nede," with "nede" suggesting both the demand for privacy and, perhaps, mounting sexual pressure (3.454). They speak only briefly about their affair, taking care that no one notices them. In any case words are hardly necessary, for their communications are perfect without them: he anticipates her every need as if "he wiste what she thoughte / Withouten word" (3.465–66). This suits her well, and indeed it should, for she has a devoted lover who has mastered the art of governance needed to preserve secrecy (3.475). He is as a wall of steel to her, precisely the kind of protection her fearful nature requires (3.479–80). And she enjoys this attention without the complications of a sexual affair.

Pandarus carries letters between them which are so numerous that the narrator recounts neither the letters nor the lovers' other exchanges. Indeed, his source has kept him from saying more, for one of these letters alone was as long as half a book, his "autour" noted, so he omitted it (3.501–3). Pandarus oversees all. Acting like Calkas "with gret deliberacioun," he has "every thyng that herto myght availle / Forncast and put in execucioun," although his objective is only to bring the lovers together at his house (3.519–21). But first Pandarus has to build a house, so to speak. "This tymbur is al redy up to frame," the narrator says (the only use of the term *frame* in Chaucer's writing), and all that is missing is knowledge of the hour Criseyde will arrive (3.530–31).

Troilus prepares for the scene in Pandarus's house by telling others that if he is not to be found, he will be praying at the temple, waiting for Apollo to communicate news of the Greeks' movements (3.544). Thus public cause provides the cover for private need. Pandarus, meanwhile, invites Criseyde to come to his house; but this takes some doing—he swears twice to underscore the need for the visit (3.556). Criseyde hesitates, for it is raining (3.562); she also asks if Troilus will be there and Pandarus swears a third time (3.570) that he is not, for if he were she would be even more frightened. Indeed, Pandarus protests that he would rather die a thousand times than have Troilus seen at his house. The narrator does not say that Criseyde believes her uncle, since his source does not say either, but her doubts are registered by the circumlocution (3.575–76). She warns Pandarus to be careful lest "goosissh" people make up stories or "dremen thynges whiche as nevere were" (3.584–85). Pandarus swears yet again that he will protect her (3.589).

The second part of book 3 discloses how honor is sacrificed when love is served. That evening, as the women gather at Pandarus's house, Troilus observes them through his own window (suggesting Criseyde's window scenes in book 2, but in much less flattering light), for he is hidden in a bath (a "stuwe" [3.601], which means "brothel") unobserved.[5] The significance of secrecy that up to this point has largely ennobled the lovers' conduct now works against Troilus, who appears to be spying and whose presence in the house compromises Criseyde and violates Pandarus's numerous oaths.

After dinner, Pandarus and Criseyde laugh and play; then suddenly, before the women depart, Fortune intervenes. Human causality is suspended as the narrator whips up a massive storm that strikes with "smoky reyn" (3.628), keeping them from leaving and reinforcing the limits Pandarus has carefully drawn around his guests. Criseyde has already remarked on this rain, and perhaps Pandarus's earlier divinations (3.551) were connected to an unusual conjunction of Jupiter and Saturn.[6] The festivities break out again, somewhat to Pandarus's frustration. He organizes the sleeping arrangements so that Criseyde can have his "litel closet," safe from the noise of the thunder (3.663), and he can sleep in an outer room; between them he puts her women, and he separates himself from them by curtains. The women's place is strategic, the deployment of a physical frame. Pandarus means them to be near Criseyde if she wants them (3.686).

When all is silent, Pandarus opens the door to the "stuwe" and lets Troilus into the room (3.698–700), telling the hero, as he climbs down, that he "shalt into hevene blisse wende" (3.704). The ironic juxtaposition of descent with ascent is appropriate to the mixed tone of the book: although sexual fulfillment is nearing for the lovers, it is purchased at the expense of truth and forthrightness.

Troilus calls for divine assistance, especially from Venus, explaining, "For nevere yet no nede / Hadde ich er now, ne halvendel the drede" (3.706–8). His call to Venus incorporates the language of the proem to this book (see 3.48), a text he echoes again later.

As the storm rages, Pandarus enters the room in which Criseyde is sleeping, commanding her to be silent. She is startled that he has found a way to enter her room without disturbing the other women, who are asleep just outside it, and he explains that a "secre trappe-dore" connects the chamber with the outer rooms (3.757–59). Criseyde wants to call others but Pandarus deters her from this rashness, saying (rather ungraciously) that it would be not wise to stir up unnecessary conjecture: "It is nought good a slepyng hound to wake, / Ne yeve a wight a cause to devyne" (3.764–65). Indeed, the women sleep so soundly that if someone undermined the house, they would not know about it (3.767). Pandarus is engaged in his own act of undermining at this point, for he tells Criseyde not only that Troilus is in the house after all but that he has heard that Criseyde "sholden love oon hatte Horaste" (3.797) and is about to die of sorrow at this betrayal.

The existence of Horaste, a false love, is another of Pandarus's fictions designed to promote a true love and to impart urgency to the tryst that he has arranged. Like many other tales he has manufactured for the same purpose, this tale associates Pandarus with the architectural metaphors that surround his acts. The story confirms some of Criseyde's worst fears; she reacts with sorrow rather than anger to learn that "my deere herte wolde me nought holde / So lightly fals!" (3.802–4). She plans to deny the story the next day and takes the occasion to make her own Boethian speech (Boethius, book 2, prose 4) about the falseness of happiness and the mutability of earthly joys. She concludes with a strong denunciation of Troilus for believing in her falseness (3.813–40). One does not know what is more surprising: that Criseyde is philosophical ("The sentiments were commonplaces," one commentator notes[7]) or that Pandarus (or the narrator) allows the long speech at so crucial a moment in the text. But it is precisely because it is a moment of tension, a crisis, that Criseyde is allowed recourse to philosophy in this exemplary way. We may resist the idea that she is an original thinker, but we should realize that she, her lover, Pandarus, and the narrator drink from the philosophical springs that feed the whole poem. Like Troilus, she has begun to argue the thesis of book 3 in her own language; for a brief moment, she has access to the same symbolic order—the Boethian ideal—that is available to him. And like him she has access to an interior where her secrets are stored, to a sense of self that does not conform to the public roles her world makes available to her.

Pandarus rejects the idea that she can postpone her explanation until the next day. Criseyde has now suggested delaying action twice—which indicates not only that she does not wish to see Troilus but that she has a gift for delaying confrontations. One does not dispute how a fire began when it has broken out: one fights it, Pandarus replies (3.855–59), and to delay would jeopardize Troilus's life. He imputes malice and foolishness to her if she allows Troilus to suffer (3.880–82). Her response is to offer Troilus her blue ring—"for ther is nothyng myghte hym bettre plese, / Save I myself" (3.886–87)—and to make another attempt to postpone the discussion until the next day. Pandarus scoffs; such a ring would have to hold a stone that could bring a dead man to life, he says (3.890–93).[8] She could put off a fool with a few words, perhaps, but not one "so gentil and so tendre of herte" on the verge of death. And it will only take "o word" to "stere" his heart, bringing the hero to rest, as it were (3.904, 3.910). Pandarus reminds her that no one knows that Troilus has come and that the knight is devoted to her, so that "bi right ye moste upon hym triste" (3.916).

The narrator renews the tone of reasonableness that Pandarus adopts to follow his high-pressure tactics. The state of things "so pitous was to here" (3.918), the narrator says, and moreover, what Pandarus has said is "so *like* a sooth at prime face"—so *like* a truth, on the face of it (my emphasis)—that Criseyde "did al for goode" in giving her consent to see Troilus (3.924). She claims that she is "at dulcarnoun, right at my wittes ende" (3.931),[9] and does not know what to do, but Pandarus smoothly assures her that her confusion is unnecessary. She insists on rising before Troilus comes to her so that she will keep her honor, but Pandarus recommends that she lie still "and taketh hym right here" (3.948), as if to address the very sexual act she seems eager to avoid.

When Troilus appears at her bedside she blushes, just as he blushed when she appeared before him in Deiphebus's house. The narrator supplies some verbal play for our benefit, using the same commonplaces to link these moments. Earlier he "wex sodeynliche red" and was so embarrassed that men "sholde smyten of his hed" (3.81, 3.82); here, she "wex sodeynliche red" and cannnot speak, though men "sholde smyten of hire hed" (3.954–57). Criseyde invites Troilus to sit instead of kneel; Pandarus approves, and taking a candle he so adjusts his countenance as if to read "an old romaunce" (3.980), when in fact he beholds a new romance of his own making.

Criseyde addresses the issue of Horaste, saying that sympathy for Troilus's pain has caused her to let him see her. There is jealousy that can be excused, for it has a cause in "som swich fantasie" and, since it can be controlled, is harmless (3.1030–34). There is also jealousy that comes from spite and fury, but that is not what Troilus suffers from. Rather, he suffers from "illusioun, / Of habundaunce of love and besy cure" (3.1041–42), and she is sorry about that but not angry (3.1049–50). This long and cogent speech puts Criseyde, a victim of shameless manipulation on the part of men, in a very good light. Nothing looks to book 5, when Troilus becomes jealous with cause, until Criseyde's eyes fill with tears, and she says, "Now God, thow woost, in thought ne dede untrewe / To Troilus was nevere yet Criseyde" (3.1053–54). The reader's eyes rest on "nevere yet."

The narrator is as engaged in events as Pandarus. "But now help God to quenchen al this sorwe!" the narrator says (3.1058), returning our attention briefly to the Christian, Chaucerian frame of past and present. Reversing the springtime rebirth Troilus has just witnessed, he cites the seasons and cycles of natural time—May follows winter, but a "misty morwe" can follow a lovely summer's day—and notes a parallel in the arts of war: victories can be expected after hard battles (3.1064). The stanza is a curious transition to Troilus's reaction. The cyclical events referred to recall the pattern of double sorrow and the unending turns of Fortune even as the affair between Troilus and Criseyde nears its zenith.

So great is Troilus's regret at Criseyde's tears that he wishes himself dead. He curses the decision to visit her there and fears that "al that labour he hath don byforn" is lost (3.1075). In his mind he denounces Pandarus's schemes and then his thoughts find words: "God woot that of this game, / Whan al is wist, than am I nought to blame" (3.1084–85). Overwhelmed, he faints. Pandarus rushes up to lift Troilus onto the bed, saying, "O thef, is this a mannes herte?" as he tears off Troilus's clothes (3.1097–99). This comic scene heavily compromises Troilus, who blames Pandarus (at least by implication) for Criseyde's misery but then collapses under his own guilt.

Criseyde, at her uncle's behest, pulls out the thorn "that stiketh in his herte" (3.1104; recalling the narrator's hope in book 2.1272–74 that she will be fixed by a thorn). She whispers her forgiveness, accompanied by oaths, and they rub his hands and temples as she kisses him. His reason returns; he is evidently embarrassed at her ministration. "Is this a mannes game?" she asks, echoing Pandarus's indignant "is this a mannes herte?" a few lines earlier (3.1097). "What, Troilus," she continues, "wol ye do thus for shame?" (3.1126–27). Pandarus withdraws to the chimney, where, to the discomfort of many of Chaucer's readers, he appears to remain during the next events. The narrator's focus stays on the bed. He notes that as Criseyde talks she loses her fear of Troilus and sees no reason to ask him to leave. The narrator cautiously comments on her protestations of good faith:

> Yet lasse thyng than othes may suffise
> In many a cas; for every wyght, I gesse,
> That loveth wel, meneth but gentilesse. (3.1146–48)

He has already observed that her oaths were not necessary (3.1142). He now suggests that she presses the charge of jealousy too hard. She insists that Troilus explain why he was jealous and what alerted him to it; if he does not explain, she will insist that "this was don of malice, hire to fonde" (that is, to test her, to find her out [3.1155]), and she is quite right. Troilus replies with a lie, however ("for the lasse harm, he moste feyne," 3.1158), saying that at a feast she failed to smile on him; the narrator dismisses this as a "rysshe," nothing but a reed, made up by someone desperate for an excuse (3.1162). Swearing "by that God that bought us bothe two" (3.1165), Criseyde too detects the foolishness of his explanation and dismisses his arguments as "naught worth a beene" and childish jealousy (3.1168–69). She offers forgiveness, warning that this must not happen again (3.1180), and then Troilus seizes her and Pandarus retires, cautioning Troilus, "If ye be wise, / Swouneth nought now, lest more folk arise!" (3.1189–90).

At this point Troilus seems predatory; the narrator resorts to a hunting image to ask what the lark feels when the hawk has caught it (3.1191–97). Criseyde trembles, but Troilus, cured of his "cares colde" (3.1202) is in command, saying, "Now be ye kaught; now is ther but we tweyne! / Now yeldeth yow, for other bote is non!" She swiftly undercuts these manly assertions: "Ne hadde I er now, my swete herte deere, / Ben yolde, ywis, I were now nought heere!" (3.1206–11). Her statement should not come as a complete surprise; it admits submissiveness at the same time that it asserts Troilus's complete dependence on her goodwill and cooperation.

Images of birds evoked earlier in hunting and trapping references emerge again in the following stanzas, which celebrate the sweetness of a love won with difficulty and the harmony that follows strife. The lovers wind their arms around one another, recalling the intertwined postures of the singing birds at the end of *The Parliament of Fowls* (666–79). As a nightingale "newe abaysed" (startled), who after some hesitation speaks, Criseyde opens her heart to Troilus (3.1233–39). He speaks of Love, Charity, and Venus, now delivering prayers at the temple of love that he has made of her rather than prayers for victory to Apollo, the prayers he expected to be making (3.544). Troilus echoes the Christian subtext of Criseyde's earlier remarks, saying, "God hath wrought me for I shall yow serve" and that she will be his "steere" (3.1290–91; compare 3.904–10). Criseyde prevents further protestations: "For it suffiseth, this that seyd is heere." She welcomes him as her knight (3.1307–9).

Reminding us of his presence, the narrator now invites the audience to judge the gladness of the lovers as they "felten in love the grete worthynesse" (that is, consummation, 3.1316). So great is their happiness that he can scarcely describe it; at the same time, however, he wants his audience to know that he has omitted nothing from his source (3.1326–27). He places all his words "under correccioun / Of yow that felyng han in loves art," deferring now to the romantic authority of the audience even to the point of allowing that audience to alter his language (3.1335–37).

The two lovers are so happy that they fear that "al this thyng but nyce dremes were," and they repeatedly ask each other if they are indeed dreaming (3.1342–44). Troilus kisses her eyes, the "humble nettes of my lady deere!" that trapped him in the temple in book 1 (3.1355). She has bound him without a bond, he says, renewing the Boethian context as he acknowledges the power of love and desire to constrain mind and heart. They exchange rings and Criseyde then attaches a gold and azure brooch, set with a ruby, to Troilus's shirt (3.1370–72). The narrator strikes out at anyone who is "a coveytous or a wrecche," for niggards cannot have "perfit joie" (3.1373–79). This strange response to the brooch seems designed to draw attention from the role it plays in book 5, when Troilus sees it on Diomede, Criseyde's Greek lover.

Troilus and Criseyde do not think of sleep, and neither does the narrator. They are occupied with the "joie and bisynesse / Of al that souneth into gentilesse" (presumably a circumlocution for sexual intercourse; 3.1413–14) when the cock sounds the arrival of morning. Concerned about her reputation, Criseyde says that she must go or be lost. She delivers a "dawn song" sung, usually, by a male lover. Chaucer reverses the roles, with Criseyde delivering the lines traditional for the male lover, and Troilus delivering the lines usually reserved for the woman.[10] The inversion of convention, an exciting illustration of sexual and emotional parity, is a powerful argument for those, including David Aers, who believe that Chaucer had a remarkably mature view of the possibilities of sexual relationships.[11] The inversion is particularly forceful because it renews and extends the earlier discussion of natural cycles (3.1064) whose force is ambiguous: spring follows winter, but autumn follows summer. The lovers denounce natural cycles and would always like to have night. This inversion of natural order is disturbing (3.1429–70), for cycles are both natural and expressive of Fortune's dominion (see 3.352, 3.617, 3.1060–64). The wish for eternal night is also a version of the Boethian cosmos, an unchanging world, a world of permanent harmony and union.

The lovers' pending separation is difficult because the terms of their union are secretive. Troilus is reluctant to go because he does not know when he will see Criseyde again (3.1478–80). He could, he tells her, accept the need to part if

> I, youre humble servant and youre knyght,
> Were in youre herte iset so fermely
> As ye in myn— (3.1489–90)

a reference that evokes her silent and uninterpreted dream of the eagle, who flew away "with herte left for herte" (2.925–31). The dream is recalled more clearly when she replies:

> That first shal Phebus fallen fro his spere,
> And everich egle ben the dowves feere,
> And everich roche out of his place sterte,
> Er Troilus oute of Criseydes herte. (3.1495–98)

She says that Troilus is "so depe in-with myn herte grave" (the image also occurs at 2.1238–41 when Pandarus speaks to her) that she will never be able to turn him out of her thoughts.

The chapter reaches its two-part conclusion with Pandarus returning, in the spirit of both author and critic, creator and framer, to assess the lovers' experiences. No sooner does Criseyde begin to reflect on the evening than Pandarus appears. "Nece, how kan ye fare," he asks. Her answer is swift and angry: "Nevere the bet for yow, / Fox that ye ben! God yeve youre herte kare!" (3.1564–65). She covers her head in embarrassment but Pandarus thrusts his hand under her neck and kisses her. "I passe al that which chargeth nought to seye," the narrator adds in an equally odd aside (3.1576); some have argued that Pandarus extracts sexual favors from Criseyde at this point, and while it is never wise to rule out ambiguity, it does seem that a woman so in possession of herself would hardly submit to so disturbing a liaison, even if when they part "Pandarus hath fully his entente" (3.1582).[12]

Troilus has sent for Pandarus; when he arrives the knight falls to his knees and thanks him for having brought his soul to rest "in hevene" from the hell of longing he had occupied (3.1599–1600). He credits Pandarus with saving his life (3.1613–14). Now joining the lovers in expressing the Boethian thesis of book 3, Pandarus warns Troilus about the fickleness of Fortune, an aspect of Boethian wisdom that does not reach Troilus's consciousness:

> For of fortunes sharpe adversitee
> The worste kynde of infortune is this,
> A man to han ben in prosperitee,
> And it remembren when it passed is.
> Th'art wis ynough; forthi do nat amys:
> Be naught to rakel, theigh thow sitte warme,
> For if thow be, certeyn it wol the harme. (3.1625–31)

Pandarus follows these lines (drawn from Boethius, book 2, prose 4), with a reminder (drawn from *The Romance of the Rose*) that it is as difficult to keep something as it is to gain it in the first place (3.1633–34).[13] Earthly joys are fragile and break easily, so it behooves Troilus to "bridle alwey wel thi speche and thi desir" (3.1635), an important image of restraint and control. Pandarus's speech about self-governance seems designed to moderate his friend's enthusiasm and his vulnerability; it is obvious that Pandarus understands more about Criseyde's need to be independent than her lover does and also that he seeks to distance Troilus a little from love's obsession.

Troilus's need for caution is revealed fully in his fulsome reply in which he declares that his desire has doubled and that his love has changed:

> I not myself naught wisly what it is,
> But now I feele a newe qualitee—
> Yee, al another than I dide er this. (3.1653–55)

Pandarus replies that naturally one's feelings change after finding the heavenly bliss that one previously only heard about. Troilus takes no heed of such moderating statements, however, and fills the rest of the day with praises of Criseyde and thanks to Pandarus. Soon thereafter the lovers meet again—Fortune wishes it to be so (3.1667)—and all is as it was the first time, at Pandarus's house. Their joy is more than the narrator can describe. "This joie may nought writen be with inke," he writes; "This passeth al that herte may bythynke" (3.1693–94). After this, they meet regularly: "Fortune a tyme ledde in joie / Criseyde and ek this kynges sone of Troie" (3.1714–15).

Book 3 concludes with a commemoration of Troilus's rejuvenated response to the affair, closely resembling his revival as victorious knight in book 1, where "ecch hym loved that loked on his face" (1.1078). At the end of book 1 he was triumphant but wounded; here he is ecstatic but bound: "of al Criseydes net" he is "narwe ymasked and yknet" so firmly that the bonds cannot be undone (3.1732–36), or so he would have it. And as he did in book 1, he becomes a poet again, singing about the bonds of the "lawe of compaignie," the "acord" of love that orders the world and creates the firmest, highest, and most lasting world imaginable. The source of this song is the same section of *The Consolation of Philosophy* (book 2, poem 8) that is the source of the invocation to book 3. Thus Chaucer's narrator and his hero, drawing from the same text, have unified their social perspectives in these celebrations of the harmonious powers of love. The conclusion asserts harmony and order. Troilus's song celebrates "a bond perpetuely durynge" (3.1754), recalling the proem, which salutes the power of Venus, the goddess who can "holden regne and hous in unitee" (3.29). But the song also acknowledges that the unifying frame can be sprung and that the vision of order can collapse in ruin:

And if that Love aught lete his bridel go,
Al that now loveth asondre sholde lepe,
And lost were al that Love halt now to-hepe. (3.1762–64)

At the moment, however, the lovers are happy. Mars is tamed by Venus. Like Venus, Criseyde is, temporarily at least, also a goddess who holds "regne and hous in unitee," but her power to unify is later undercut in book 4, when the forces of war—Mars untamed—turn on Venus and destroy the lovers' happiness. The final lines of book 3 elaborate the symbiosis between the hero's numerous virtues and his martial skills. Troilus smiles on lovers whom he once mocked and considers those who are not in love little more than lost (3.1793–95). He is also "the first in armes dyght" (3.1773), and, when there is respite from war, he exercises his hunting skills, although—newly gentle—he spares small animals (3.1779–81). The narrator concludes with repeated thanks to Cupid, calling the book his own song ("I seyd fully in my song / Th'effect and joie of Troilus servise," 3.1814–15). Despite "som disese among, / As to myn auctour listeth to devise," the lovers are happy "in lust and in quiete" (3.1819). At this point, then, Troilus enjoys the perspective of the Boethian philosopher, the courtly lover, and the individual who has achieved sexual and psychological peace. He views the affair from each of these frames, conscious of each in a way that no other character in the poem is. Now movement from "woe" to "wel" is complete, and there remains only, after a period of continued bliss, a descent that will destroy these perspectives and supplant them, in book 5, with one far colder and more distant. The chain of love is the reign "that knetteth lawe of compaignie" (3.1748) and that "cerclen hertes alle and faste bynde" (3.1767). If we compare Troilus's speech to *The Consolation of Philosophy*, we see how cleverly Chaucer stages his hero's adaptation of the text. In the original Lady Philosophy is warning Boethius *away from* trust in earthly love; Troilus does exactly the opposite as he uses the poem to confirm that very same attachment. The "pure love" mentioned by Lady Philosophy is not what Troilus is thinking of; all his thoughts are on Criseyde. He finds that his tie to Criseyde outlasts her tie to him. The well-being that pervades the poem at this point does not derive only from their happiness in sexual union. Troilus and Criseyde have fallen in love; more importantly, they have, in the Boethian symbolic frame of the poem, fallen into place.

8

Coming Apart:
Book 4 and the War

War governs book 4 as absolutely as love frames book 3. Love and war are fitting pairs of frames for these two books, frames Chaucer superimposes alternately and sometimes simultaneously after this point. The "quiet motions" of the Boethian text that is the source of the proem to book 3 are torn apart in book 4 when the demands of war force the Trojans to revalue Criseyde, abandon their promise to protect her, and agree to exchange her for captured Trojan warriors. The war returns her to the dangerous status she held at the opening of the poem. Not unexpectedly, it is her character that shifts the most when the frame of unifying love is replaced by the order of war. Pandarus, ever the realist, remains pragmatic, and Troilus, at the end of book 4, is a rigid idealist still. But Criseyde is not the same, especially in her long discussion with Troilus about her future. In this book she is far more assertive and directed than she was before or will be again; in the discourse of the frame of war she stands alone and, for a time, speaks for herself.

Book 4 begins with the shortest, and the last, of the proems. The narrator announces that Fortune, "that semeth trewest whan she wol bygyle / And kan to fooles so hire song entune" (4.3–4), has turned from Troilus and begun to favor Diomede, Criseyde's lover-to-be instead (4.11). Reluctant to explain how Criseyde abandons her lover, the narrator assumes a protective stance. He first says that she "forsook" him, but he immediately softens this: "Or at the leeste, how that she was unkynde," adding that those who speak ill of her "hemself sholde han the vilanye" (4.15–16, 4.21). The narrator now calls on the Furies to aid him, invoking Thesiphone, the muse who presided over the first proem, "so that the losse of lyf and love yfeere / Of Troilus be fully shewed heere" (4.27–28). Book 4, with its greatly expanded frame, shows us more than Troilus and his misery: for the first time since book 1 we glimpse the political world of Troy, the magnitude of the war, and the operations of the public world that the lovers have excluded from their bliss.

The narrator has already attributed the reversal of Troilus's happiness to Fortune, but as book 4 begins the human cause is located among the Trojans and their war. They fight poorly and sustain a significant defeat on the battlefield: "The folk of Troie hemselven so mysledden / That with the worse at nyght homward they fledden" (4.48–49). Several of their most important knights are taken prisoner, including Antenor, and the losses in Troy are great: "that day the folk of Troie / Dredden to lese a gret part of hire joie" (4.55–56). Fear of losing the war becomes widespread; a general sense of alarm signals a new and conspicuous role for the Trojan public in the poem. The Greeks request a truce (in Chaucer's source they ask this so that they can bury their dead), which King Priam grants.

In the Greek camp Calkas hears of the truce and speaks to a gathering of the Greek lords. He reminds them that he was the first to tell them of their eventual triumph over the Trojans and that he has given them strategies for taking the town (4.78–80). Now Calkas has come to ask something for himself: he wants his daughter. Taking a moment to indulge in fatherly sentiments ("O sterne, O cruel fader that I was!" [4.94]), he proposes that since so many Trojans have been captured, one of them should be exchanged for Criseyde (4.108). He has been told by Apollo and "be astronomye" (4.113–15) that the city shall be destroyed by the anger of Apollo and Neptune (who built and blessed the walls but who were not paid for their work by Laomedon).[1] The Greeks are moved by the old man's tears and agree to exchange Antenor for his daughter. Greek ambassadors take the proposal to Priam's "parlement." Troilus is in attendance and is therefore among the first to hear of the pending exchange. By now experienced at suppressing his emotions in public, he betrays no sign in speech or act; instead he immediately begins deciding how to resist the proposal and save Criseyde's honor (4.158–60).

Love and Reason personified debate within him, Love counseling him to prevent the exchange and Reason warning him to do nothing without consulting Criseyde, for if he acts he may advertise their love to the world, "ther it was erst unknowe" (4.168). Thus the demand for silence continues to constrain the lovers in woe, just as it has restricted them in happiness. Already there is opposition from Hector to Criseyde's exchange; he reminds the Greeks that since she is not a prisoner, the only means of transferring her would be to sell her to them, and he adds, "We usen here no wommen for to selle" (4.182). But public opinion denounces his view. "Ector," the people say, "what goost may yow enspyre / This womman thus to shilde and don us leese / Daun Antenor" (4.187–89). To Priam they say, "al oure vois is to forgon Criseyde" (to forfeit her) and to have Antenor instead (4.196). The narrator ridicules their view and comments on the irony that they want to deliver Antenor, "that brought hem to meschaunce" (4.203). When he removed the statue of Pallas from Troy (see 1.153), "he was after traitour to the town" (4.203–4). But the parliament agrees with the people: Criseyde must go.

The social world that has, up to this point, barely existed in the poem now unites against the lovers and conspires against Criseyde. Daughter of a traitor, subject to Priam and the parliament, she has become a public liability. The poem makes little of the pattern, but the power flowing around her is distributed according to gender. Criseyde's value in the symbolic system is now multiplied. To her father she is mere chattel. He claims to want her rather than the treasure he left behind; later he reveals that he expects his daughter to come with many possessions. To Hector she is embarrassingly controversial, the reminder of a promise his people will not allow him to keep. To Troilus, she is also a sign—but to him she is an emblem of his own promises to her, promises that he will keep. What is she to herself, the reader may wonder—the sign of a promise she cannot keep?

Troilus returns to his room, and the metaphors of the cycles of the seasons and the ship once again signal his condition. He is like a tree bereft of leaves in winter, "ibounden in the blake bark of care" (4.225–31). Like a raging bull, he beats his head against the wall, weeps, and asks for death—acts that replay, with new and grim intensity, the emotional outbursts that followed his first sight of Criseyde. He attacks "unkynde" Fortune (4.266) for his fall into misery and asks why Fortune has not taken someone's life—his father's or his brother's, or his own, for whatever he has done wrong (4.276–80). If he could be with Criseyde, he would not care where Fortune would steer their boat (4.282), but without her he will be lost. His death wish takes the form of the soul's flight: he asks his soul to "unneste," to leave the nest of the body, and to fly after Criseyde (4.305–7). This is a figure that reappears at the end of this book and that looks ahead to his soul's flight to the eighth sphere in book 5.

In the manner of the narrator, Troilus addresses all lovers, asking that when they see his sepulchre they remember him as their "felawe" (4.328). Then he denounces Calkas and sinks into a trance in which Pandarus, who has also heard the decree in parliament, finds him. Pandarus shares this experience with Troilus as if it is happening to him as well. Fortune has overthrown "oure joie," he says, "hire yiftes ben comune," and no one can trust her (4.385, 4.391–92). But Pandarus immediately reverts to his practical perspective, urging Troilus to accept the decision since "thi desir al holly hastow had, / So that, by right, it oughte ynough suffise" (4.395–96). The city is full of beautiful women, he continues, and "if she be lost, we shal recovere an other" (4.401–6). Pandarus's advice resembles that of the goose in *The Parliament of Fowls*: "But she wol love hym, lat hym love another!" (567) or that of the duck: "There been mo sterres, God wot, than a payre!" (595). Pandarus offers comparably chaotic and amoral consolations, revealing how little he values Troilus's idealistic view of love. Troilus ignores Pandarus: "Oon ere it herde, at tother out it wente" (4.434). He says that such "lechecraft" would be treason unto one who is true to him (4.436–38) and that he will be Criseyde's until he dies (4.444). Right about himself, he is wrong about her.

But Troilus has been paying close attention to Pandarus, for he refutes his friend's advice point for point, missing no opportunity to denounce the pragmatism and falseness Pandarus has advised. Recalling the arrow of the god of love in book 1, Troilus insists that Criseyde's "dart" shall never leave his heart (4.472–73). He uses his friend's advice against him. If women are so easy to find, why doesn't Pandarus find another for himself? Who is Pandarus to give advice if he is unhappy in love himself? (4.484–97). Pandarus ventures to suggest that Troilus either "ravysshe" her—that is, carry her away by force—or insist that she stay; he challenges the hero to "kith [make known] thow art a man" (4.538).

Troilus's systematic refutation of Pandarus's position signals an organized, intelligent nature and the character of one who knows how to argue. First, Troilus says, the war has been caused by a rape, and to take Criseyde by force would be wrong, for the Trojans generally agreed that "she is chaunged for the townes goode." Second, his father, Priam, has agreed to the exchange, and the king's word cannot be repealed (4.553–60). Third, he does not want to upset Criseyde and create scandal about her. He concludes that he is lost, "with desir and reson twight," pulled one way by the desire to take her and pulled another way by reason, which forbids that he do so (4.572–74). Pandarus replies that if he himself were as much in love as Troilus is, he would take Criseyde away and let the town be outraged, for what people shout about today they will whisper about tomorrow. Suggesting that the scandal will pass (4.586–88), Pandarus becomes the first speaker in the poem both to consider the possibility of scandal and also to dismiss it.

Pandarus counsels aggression as well as disobedience when he returns to the example of Paris, which, he suggests, Troilus could emulate. He argues that if Criseyde loves Troilus as much as he loves her, she will not object to aggressive acts on her behalf, and if she does, her uncle says ungraciously enough, "Thanne is she fals; so love hire wel the lasse" (4.616). "Thorugh love is broken al day every lawe," Pandarus concludes (4.618), revealing precisely how the frame of book 3 relates to the frame of book 4: love must assert order because lawlessness (war, deception) is its other side. Troilus hesitates, vowing no action without Criseyde's consent. Pandarus tells Troilus to keep up appearances and to return to the king, lest he be asked for, but to dissimulate, "with wisdom hym and othere blende" or deceive (4.648). Events remain in Pandarus's control; he arranges a meeting between Troilus and Criseyde for later that evening, so that their final night together, like their first, takes place under Pandarus's roof.

Word of the exchange flies through Troy. Finally Criseyde hears it; her response is to reject her father, for whom she cares little and whose death would not trouble her (4.666–68). Caught like Troilus between love and fear, she dares not ask about the details of the arrangement. The narrator is at pains to underscore her love for Troilus and to say that she would not, for all the world, "Troilus out of hire herte caste" (4.676). Her retinue and friends surround her with good wishes, expecting that she will be happy to be rejoining her father and also hoping that her departure will bring peace. Even though they stand next to her, they are far from her, and she from them; her body sits among the women but her soul seeks her lover (4.699). In this group of women Criseyde is, in a rare moment, seen outside her usual place in the sexual or courtly symbolic order: she is superior to most of the company, but her identity among them is that of daughter, not lover. There are "only" women here, with no men present to assign them places in the symbolic order. This is not a powerful community but rather merely a shadow of the real parliament, where power flows and lives are managed.

When the women leave, Criseyde returns to her room and becomes a figure of despair, tearing her hair and cursing her fate and the day she first saw Troilus (4.743–49). She calls on both her hitherto unmentioned mother, Argyve, and on her father, blaming him for this development and cursing the day of her birth (4.761–63). This curse is followed by unnatural images: without Troilus she is a fish out of water and a plant without a root. That is, without her natural surroundings to nourish her, she will die: she says that she will refuse food and starve, since she cannot carry a sword and meet a more violent end (as Troilus can and will; 4.771–77). The "law of kynde" operates as Criseyde talks about the nourishment of love in terms of simple physical dependence. But her concerns, compared with those of Troilus, are pragmatic and practical, and the unnatural images are too severe to be maintained. Criseyde will live, but she will swim in different water. She imagines that she will don black clothes, and her religious "ordre" until she dies "shal sorwe ben, compleynt, and abstinence" (4.778–84). She has already been seen in the black habit of a widow and has jokingly referred to herself as an anchoress in book 2; now she will wear black as the "tokenyng" of sorrow and behave like a nun. But if this is too self-dramatizing, and seems insincere, we should remember that war has reduced her to the helpless, friendless status she dreaded in book 1 when her father left Troy. Now, without communal support to protect her status in the social order, she must temporarily redefine her place in the symbolic order. In book 5 she reverts to the type in which the symbolic order casts her. In book 4, the poem permits her a small show of strength.

Several details in Criseyde's monologue parallel Troilus's speech earlier in this book. For example, she leaves her body and soul to him; her black clothes recall his wish for the darkness of hell (4.473–74). She will be "chaunged" for Antenor, she says, and here she is right, although the changes are not those she expects. First, she will be "chaunged" in that she will take the advice Pandarus gives Troilus and will find a new lover, exchanging Troilus for Diomede. Second, the speech recalls her dream in which she and the eagle exchange hearts. The motif of the exchange of hearts emerges in Criseyde's subsequent speech (4.785–98), where we find two meanings for her repeated "herte myn": "Myn herte" (4.785) meaning her own heart, "herte myn" (4.792) meaning Troilus. Third, because she has been disfigured by sorrow, her hair undone, her color gone, she is "transmewed" in woe (4.830). When Pandarus sees her, she does not know whether she should welcome him or not, for the happiness he brought her has now turned to sorrow (4.828–33). Indeed, she believes that she embodies it: "Whoso me seeth, he seeth sorwe al atonys— / Peyne, torment, pleynte, wo, distresse!" (4.841–42). Criseyde's response resembles Troilus's in many ways, but there is a single, key difference: she regards the exchange, from the first (as early as 4.780), with fatalistic acceptance. When she asks if Troilus will have "pleynte or teris" when she leaves, it is clear that her departure is inevitable (4.860).

Pandarus proceeds with his plan to bring the two together at his house that evening and he wants her to be more cheerful when she sees Troilus. She replies that her lover's sorrow worsens her own; "his sorwe doubleth al my peyne" (4.903), she says, thus creating her own "double sorrow." Here too the narrator raises an ominous implication, for although it is difficult for her to go, it is even more difficult for her to see Troilus's sorrow, her "bane" (4.905–7). One wonders if she will leave in part to remove herself from his grief. We are prepared for her betrayal here, since the clear implication in her speech is "out of sight, out of mind," a line of thinking explicitly advocated by Pandarus in his earlier discussion with Troilus. Pandarus reminds her that she must help Troilus become strong, not worsen his condition, and that she should plan how to prevent her departure or arrange for her return after she departs. Pandarus has suggested the course that the lovers will take and that will lead to desertion (4.934–35).

Criseyde sends Pandarus to Troilus, whom he finds in a temple rehearsing the conditions of his destruction. In this extremely long and difficult speech, which continues for some 120 lines (4.958–1082), Troilus supplies a bumbling version of Boethius's discussion of fate and free will (Boethius, book 5, prose 2 and 3).[2] In permitting the hero a confused philosophical dissertation at a crucial point in the plot, Chaucer took a considerable artistic risk. The length of Troilus's meditation is difficult to justify, and the speech is riddled with signs of its own tedium—for example, "now herkne, for I wol nat tarie" (4.1029). One wonders who "harkens" to this discussion. Demonstrating highly selective knowledge of Boethius, Troilus completes his imperfect movement through *The Consolation of Philosophy*. In Boethius, the binding force of universal order and harmony is invoked immediately before a long discussion of free will (Boethius, book 5, poem 1). Troilus now takes up this subject, but he omits the most important point in the text, the reply that Lady Philosophy makes in defense of the position Boethius takes.[3] Philosophy reminds Boethius that human reason cannot comprehend the simplicity of divine foreknowledge: "For just as knowledge of things happening now does not imply necessity in their outcomes, so foreknowledge of future things imposes no necessity on their outcomes in the future" (Boethius, book 5, prose 4).

Pandarus's reaction to the speech anticipates the response of many readers: "I! Who say evere a wis man faren so?" (4.1086). Troilus seems to regard Criseyde's departure as an accomplished fact, prompting Pandarus to revert to his earlier, cynical mode. He accuses Troilus of acting as though he were born for one woman only and of giving up without discovering if anything can be done to prevent her departure (4.1100–1106). He directs Troilus to talk to Criseyde and look for a happy solution, and Troilus agrees. Their final meeting at Pandarus's house elaborately recalls their first meeting, but now it is Criseyde who swoons, a reference to Troilus's fainting in book 3 so pointed that one feels it cannot be accidental. Her spirit leaves her body (departs from "his propre place," 4.1152) and she lies as if dead. Troilus believes that she has died and prays for her soul; he arranges her cold body for burial and draws his own sword, planning to kill himself and send his soul after hers (4.1180–90). Then he calls on Atropos, one of the three Furies whom the narrator invoked to preside over this book (4.1208). As he raises his sword, she sighs his name, he kisses her, and "hire goost, that flikered ay o-lofte, / Into hire woful herte ayeyn it wente" (4.1221–22). Criseyde rises from this "deathbed" newly strong, deliberate, and decisive, if only for a time.

In a long section that takes the form of a debate, Criseyde raises the issue of her departure: "To fynde boote of wo that we ben inne, / It were al tyme soone to bygynne" (4.1259–60). Seizing the initiative, she becomes a woman "avysed sodeynly" who has found "art ynough" to help them avoid disaster. She echoes Pandarus's advice to her, that women "ben wise in short avysement" (4.936), and pragmatic wisdom proves to be Criseyde's strength as she and Troilus discuss the crisis. She proposes that she leave but return to Troy within one or two weeks. Her departure is the decree of parliament and cannot be prevented, so the idea of not going must be put "out of mynde" (4.1301). Since there is a truce, he will have news of her regularly, and she will not be "hid in muwe," that is, in a trap (such as Troilus hid in on their first meeting; 4.1310). If they follow her plan, she will return before the truce is suspended, and "thanne have ye both Antenore ywonne / And me also," she says, as if Troilus were concerned about the other warrior (4.1315–16). She expects to return within 10 days (4.1320).

Criseyde notes that they are, after all, used to separations. In order to keep their love a secret, they already have been apart for nearly two weeks at a time (4.1325–27); thus a separation of 10 days will not be so serious an interruption. In any case, she will have to return to Troy, for all her family save her father are there (this family has not been much in evidence up to this point), but most of all she will return because of Troilus (4.1334–35). Her father wrongly thinks that she is despised in Troy because of what he has done; if he knew that she was happy, he would not want to disturb her (4.1338–41). She stresses that peace is near; there is talk that Helen will be returned—an example Criseyde does well to cite, given its relevance to her own case (4.1347)—and that peace and freedom are near. But whether or not there is peace, she will

return (4.1360–61). And, she says, in the middle of an extensive re-
hearsal of options that she has prepared in a very short time, there
are other strategies to think about.

She turns again to her father, this time with great cynicism. He
is covetous and she knows how to trap him. "Withouten net, wher-
with I shal hym hente," she says (4.1371–72), evoking the references to traps and nets that have figured into the love affair. She
will take her possessions—"moeble"—to him and say that they have
been sent by his friends, who hope he will send for more, since Troy
is "in jupartie" (4.1380–86). Only she can take such "an huge
quantite" from Troy; she will use the wealth to demonstrate that
she is held in the court's favor and that her friends have soothed
Priam's anger at Calkas's treason, so that he can now return to the
city. She will "so enchaunten" with her "sawes" (stories) "that right
in hevene his sowle is, shal he mete" (shall he dream), she says.
Apollo, or "his clerkes lawes, / Or calkullynge, avayleth nought thre
hawes" against her scheme, she is sure, for "desir of gold" will fool
him completely (4.1390–1400). If he argues with her, she will
contradict him, convince him that the gods speak "in am-
phibologies," or ambiguities, and that the gods lie. She does not
doubt that she can persuade her father to agree to her plan
quickly, "withinne a day or tweye" (4.1413). Criseyde has few scru-
ples about deceiving her father. The narrator, as if reacting to this
exposure of her manipulative behavior, inserts a long apology—not
for the speech we have just heard but for her eventual failure to do
as she has just promised. The narrator says that she spoke with
"good entente, / And that hire herte trewe was and kynde," that she
was "in purpos evere to be trewe," and that he finds testimony to
her fidelity in separate books (4.1415–21). Curiously, the only
books we have about her from Chaucer or his English successors
attest to her infidelity and its punishment.

This remarkable section demonstrates Criseyde's skill as a political strategist, her self-confidence, and her awareness of her
newfound powers of persuasion. If the war reveals her weaknesses
anew, it also uncovers her considerable strengths. She clearly out-
performs the lover who ought to be a source of strength to her. Her
speech is uncharacteristic of her place in the symbolic order; confident and self-assured, she emerges here as an acute observer of the
political realities that confront the lovers. Troilus agrees with her,

with some misgivings; he takes her departure "for the beste" (4.1428) and the lovers temporarily return to happiness, sunshine, and even bird song. But Troilus cannot put her departure out of his mind and warns her that she will be "unkynde," unnatural, if she does not return and that he will slay himself if she delays, for there is no guarantee that her "sleghtes" will work. Then he adds that the bear thinks one thing while his trainer thinks another; that one can outrun the wise but not outwit them; and that it is difficult to limp undetected before a cripple (4.1456–58). Troilus's reversion to proverbial lore here is also out of character: this is one of the few sections in which he speaks a succession of proverbs. But he too speaks with political insight. Even if there is peace, he says, Calkas has so soiled his own reputation in Troy that he will never be able to return. Troilus also doubts that Criseyde can outsmart her father, who will talk her into becoming a wife (4.1471–72) and will praise some Greek and "ravysshen" her with his speech, or force her to do what he wants, and, in effect, detain her by force as Troilus has been refusing to do (4.1473–77). In addition, there will be many handsome men among the Greeks who will shame the "rudenesse" of the "sely Troians" and test her loyalty. He fears that her plan might fail, a prospect that threatens to rip the soul from his breast—a return of the motif of the soul's flight (4.1493). He pleads with her to run away with him; he observes that they have treasure enough to live happily until death.

Criseyde reviews his ideas, dismissing his fears as baseless. She will never be false to him, she insists, and deserves to be mad if she is (4.1535–40). She piles up oaths to testify to her fidelity. If she is false, let the river Symois return to its source and let her sink "body and soule" into hell (4.1550–54). It would be foolish and even dangerous for Troilus to leave his friends and the city that needs his help so badly. As she counters his political arguments with appeals to honor, she supports the arguments that necessitate her departure. She juxtaposes the claims of the social system, in which Troilus stands as an important warrior, against the symbolic system, in which he stands as her protector. She points out that if he deserted he could never return, for the people would denounce him as a coward and would not believe that love inspired his departure (he has already made a similar argument about her father; 4.1564–73).

Criseyde's demonstration of logic and political acumen in this episode reflects strength and sense. But not all readers agree. David Aers argues that Criseyde's speech "downgrades the full heterosexual love of a man for a woman in relation to inter-male friendship and the cohesion of the male aristocracy"; he adds that she also "downgrades women," placing war over love and accepting "crude militaristic notions" of honor. He takes her arguments as indications that she has internalized "anti-feminist norms" in defense of a male-dominated ideology.[4] Aers's reading has implications for Chaucer's achievement, of course, since Aers credits Chaucer with portraying the inability of a woman to escape a male point of view. Criseyde seems to demonstrate how patriarchy is defended by women as well as by men. But Criseyde's ability to "read like a man," in Dinshaw's words (Dinshaw, 51, 54), or to "think like a man," demonstrates more than her domination by a hostile social system. In book 3, both Criseyde and Troilus demonstrated the power of love to enable lovers to change places, to reverse roles. In book 4 this freedom continues so long as the secret, private world of love supplies the interior discursive space that the freedom requires.

Criseyde's views at this point are not entirely concentrated on Troilus, in any case. There is also her own reputation to consider, how with "filthe it spotted sholde be" if she left with him (4.1578). Rather than steal away, they should "maketh vertu of necessite" (4.1586), advice borrowed from "The Knight's Tale" (see I, 3042). Fortune only intimidates the weak, she adds, using a version of Pandarus's earlier argument that Fortune aids the strong (4.600). She concludes with additional protestations of her devotion and again mentions that she will return on the tenth day, in effect setting a calendar against which Troilus will measure both her fidelity to her intentions and his own suffering (4.1597–99). When he again suggests that they run away together, she seems almost angry at his lack of trust in her, but she revealingly includes among her oaths an oath to Cynthia, goddess of the moon and of mutability (4.1604–10).

I have been arguing that in this book, framed by war, and in the last one, framed by love, Criseyde and Troilus are free to reverse roles, to change places within the symbolic system of Boethian love that keeps them in place. A further sign of this freedom, born of an equitable sexual and psychological relationship, is that *she* admonishes *him* to ignore other lovers while she is away. "For I am evere agast," she says, "forwhy men rede / That love is thyng ay ful of bisy drede" (4.1644–45). No woman would be more betrayed than she if he were to do so, and she asks him not to be "unkynde," the word that has already been attached to her departure by Troilus and that he attaches to her betrayal in the next book. He now supplies the promises of fidelity that she has made so often (4.1653–59). Softening, she replies that she is also bound to him and has been from the first. Her interest in him is not motivated by his royal estate, his worthiness, or his nobility, she says, although we know that these are the very attributes that first caught her attention in the window scenes in book 2. Instead, "moral vertu, grounded upon trouthe," explains why she first took pity on her lover (4.1672–73). With this strikingly false claim, she sends him on his way. Her subsequent praise of his moderation and self-control rings true, but Troilus knows that she cannot remain in Troy. He leaves her chamber, and his soul, as if in sympathy, leaves his heart (4.1700).

War raises Criseyde's self-preservation instincts to a high level and places Troilus (quite literally) on the defensive. There is a war of words between the lovers now, a serious disagreement that spells the end of their happiness and that could possibly have altered their relations permanently even if Criseyde had remained in Troy. In book 4 the frame of war causes a temporary reversal of their roles: the idealist never at a loss for words cannot refute the arguments of his lover, a woman of measured speech, who commands a powerful, politically astute point of view completely at odds with her place in the symbolic order (although readers who agree with Aers will see that her arguments only confirm her repressed position). In book 5, however, this reversal itself is reversed, and she once again becomes the powerless figure whose exchange value depends entirely on her exclusion from the power structures that drive the social system in which she exists.

9

Lost in Space: Book 5 and Fate

Book 4 closes with Troilus's sensation of "dethes cares colde" (4.1692) at Criseyde's pending and unpreventable departure. This image of finality corroborates events that cannot be circumvented and establishes the tone of the final book of the poem, which is framed by fate—that which dooms human actors through causes outside their control. I have framed previous books either with mediators or with forces guiding human actions. For book 5 I have selected a frame that seems to control all else: fate. This frame has been present from the first lines, which tell us that the poem's course of events is already known.

It seems as if the gods ordain events in the poem, or, if we operate within the narrator's fourteenth-century frame of past and present, as if the Christian God wills them. It hardly matters which god we consider, for if every historical condition has an immediate cause it also has numerous remote causes whose origins are beyond the recall of memory. Both symbolic and social systems, no matter how natural they seem, have had historical beginnings. But such systems are not invented wholesale so much as they are slowly developed and gradually inherited through a process virtually imperceptible to those who exist within them. The conditions of the Trojan War were not, strictly speaking, outside human control: had Paris not run away with Helen, Agamemnon would not have laid siege to the city. Likewise, conditions in the poem seem to be

114

produced by human actors. Calkas has asked for his daughter, and the Greeks and Trojans have agreed to an exchange of prisoners that involves her. But here too human will and desire are repeatedly shown to be powerless against the force of destiny. When Cassandra expounds the dreams of Troilus in book 5, the events of his life seem to be inextricable from the doings of those long dead. It is fate in this sense of developments that cannot be arrested, events that cannot be avoided, confrontations that cannot be evaded, that frames book 5.

This book begins more simply and more darkly than any other. Alone of the five books of *Troilus and Criseyde* it has no proem or introduction, and, perhaps as a consequence, alone of the five its frame is, until the conclusion, unobtrusive. The commentary that precedes the first four books is supplied here by the palinode, which invokes multiple contexts for the work—religious, philosophical, moral, and historical. Chaucer's framing strategy has a simple rationale. In the first place, the course of book 5 has been known from the first lines of the poem. In the second place, the Muses abandoned the poem at the close of book 3 (3.1811–12); the spirits introduced to guide the poem thereafter were Tisiphone, Megaera, and Alecto, the three Furies (4.24). Presiding over book 5 are the three Fates: Clotho, Lachesis, and Atropos (the latter of whom has been mentioned twice in the previous book; see 4.1208 and 4.1546). This three-stage shift of presiding figures—from those who inspire poetry, to those who seek vengeance, and finally to those who control destiny and cut the thread of life—suitably measures the darkening landscape of the poem. The disaster that the book narrates is too well known to require an introduction; its course is already fixed, already framed.

Somewhat to our surprise we now learn how much time has passed during this story: there have been three winters and three springs since Hecuba's son, Troilus, began to love Criseyde (5.8–14). On the day of her departure, Troilus and Criseyde leave the city gates in dejection. From the opposite direction Diomede rides out eagerly to meet her, his readiness sharply contrasted to the lovers' reluctance (5.20–25). Troilus, the narrator warns us, will never see Criseyde in Troy again (5.27–28). But the hero conceals his despair and preserves the silence and secrecy that have ruled their conduct. When he sees Diomede he shakes with anger and excoriates himself for failing to prevent the exchange. He contemplates killing Diomede—whose name, significantly, he knows (5.46)—but does not because Criseyde might be harmed as a result.

Antenor comes forth to greet Troilus with a kiss that conceals the hero's desire to weep (5.75–77). The ensuing contrast between Diomede and Troilus offers two views of the symbolic system in which Criseyde exists: the hero's idealized version, and his competitor's cool, practical interpretation of the same circumstances. Skilled in matters social and sexual, Diomede notes the strain when Troilus silently hands over the bridle of Criseyde's horse (5.85–91). Diomede immediately begins to seek for "a meene" to approach Criseyde; but, knowing that time will work in his favor, he moves slowly (5.99–105). Diomede's search for "a meene" parallels Troilus's need for Pandarus, the "meene" who operated "bitwixen game and ernest" in book 3 (3.254–56). Troilus required another's assistance; Diomede will find his own way. Diomede speaks casually to Criseyde as they ride, offering to do what he can for her and promising that the Greeks will honor her just as the Trojans have (5.118–19): "A Grek ye sholde among us alle fynde / As any Troian is, and ek as kynde" (5.125–26). (At this point the Greeks will easily seem kinder to her than the Trojans have been.) He asks to serve her as her brother (4.134) but, having seemingly allayed her fears of romantic interest with this word, he adds that the Trojans and Greeks together serve one god of love (5.141–43). As they near her father's tent, he boldly asks for her hand and, with a courtly flourish, says that he is, so long as his life lasts, hers—"youre owene aboven every creature" (5.154). Similar courtly commonplaces stud his ensuing conversation (5.148–75). He makes a charming if insincere impression; he is, the narrator has told us, someone who knows what is best for himself ("he that koude his good," 5.106).

The contrast to Troilus's behavior in the first two books is instructive: Diomede is both unthreatening (offering service as a sibling— exactly the kind of relationship Criseyde first offered Troilus [see 2.1223–24])—and impressive as a courtly lover. Criseyde's response is likewise double-edged. She hears only "a word or two" but also gives signs of having heard much more:

> But natheles she thonketh Diomede
> Of al his travaile and his goode cheere,
> And that hym list his frendshipe hire to bede;

116

And she accepteth it in good manere,
And wol do fayn that is hym lief and dere,
And tristen hym she wolde, and wel she myghte,
As seyde she; and from hire hors sh'alighte. (5.183–89)

It appears that she knows how to respond without listening; but in fact she has listened and takes pains to return Diomede's goodwill. Her meeting with Calkas, in comparison, is perfunctory. He embraces her and kisses her "twenty tyme," but she says only that she was "fayn with hym to mete." For the rest she is "muwet, milde, and mansuete"—silent, mild, and meek (5.191–94). The scene is without pathos or narrative interest; the focus is not on the cause of the exchange itself but on its consequences.

The narrator quickly turns to Troilus, who has reverted to the emotional extremes of book 1. He dreams the first of two dreams that parallel Criseyde's two dreams in book 2. In the first he dreams that, having fallen into the hands of his enemies, he is alone "in place horrible"; he cries out as if he has fallen from aloft—fallen out of place, just as she has—and then he weeps (5.246–59). The narrator, now directly addressing the "redere," declares that no one can justly describe the hero's sorrows (5.270–71), but when Pandarus, who has had to stay close to the king, visits Troilus, we find that Troilus describes his sorrows well indeed. He has begun to plan his funeral because his dreams, "now and yore ago," have told him that he "mot nedes dye" (5.317–18). He makes a will: his shield is to be given to Pallas (an ironic image, since Troilus has been the shield to another Pallas, his own goddess Criseyde [5.306–8]); his horses, to Mars; and his ashes, to Criseyde. Predictably impatient with his friend's sentimental and fatalistic attitude, Pandarus responds with an attack on dreams that calls to mind Pertelote's refutation of Chauntecleer's dreams in "The Nun's Priest's Tale" (VII, 4098–4159). Once more dreams raise the larger issue of fate and free will that was dealt with extensively, and inconclusively, in the previous book. Troilus's belief in dreams serves as an excuse not to act, and that refusal triggers Pandarus's impatience.

Pandarus urges Troilus to allow time to work its cure; separations cannot be prevented and people part "of necessite" (5.339). Other unfortunate people, those who see their lovers married "by frendes myght," by the power of friends that cannot be resisted, simply accept such separations and endure the sorrow that comes with them. Such reversals are painful, but time heals them, he adds, implying that equally unavoidable public pressure has undone the "marriage" of Troilus and Criseyde (5.344–50). Pandarus seems to be telling Troilus to endure only 10 days, but in fact he may be addressing the much larger question of Criseyde's permanent removal from the city. He ridicules the significance of the dreams—they are merely "ordure" (5.385)— and he recommends that they visit Sarpedon (who was taken prisoner and presumably has been released, perhaps as part of the exchange involving Antenor). The exhortation to rise (5.393, 5.407) is emblematic of reversing the fall of Troilus's fortunes. Troilus agrees: since he must rise, rise he shall (5.421–22). Language also evokes the pattern of fortune: they speak "up and down" about visiting Sarpedon and then go to a splendid feast at the king's house, where royal, courtly splendor forms a stark contrast to the despair Troilus seeks to leave behind. The music played at the feast makes him sad. Since the woman "that of his herte berth the keye" is away, he thinks that no one should "maken melodie" (5.459–62). The sexual subtext is a significant indicator of his loss of perspective; it is unreasonable to expect that, since Troilus and Criseyde are apart, others should not be together.

Troilus occasionally thinks that he sees Criseyde; he hauls out her old letters and reads them in order to reimagine her. And thus he passes his time up to the fourth day. He is eager to be alone with his sorrows— in this and in numerous other ways Troilus behaves as many lovers still do—but Pandarus says that, since they have promised to spend a week at the feast, they cannot leave without giving offense (5.491–97). When they do leave at the end of a week, Troilus bursts into song. He expects Criseyde back quickly, but Pandarus is not so optimistic, rightly doubting that Calkas will be eager to send Criseyde at all (5.505–8).

The day after their return, Troilus visits Criseyde's house. He sees the barred doors and closed windows—the windows he rode before twice in book 2, once in triumph, once in subjugation. He apostrophizes the house:

> O paleys desolat,
> O hous of houses whilom best ihight,
> O paleys empty and disconsolat,

118

O thow lanterne of which queynt is the light,
O paleys, whilom day, that now art nyght,
Wel oughtestow to falle, and I to dye,
Syn she is went that wont was us to gye! (5.540–46)

The uncomfortable but by now familiar pun on "queynt" merges sexual subtext with the narrative imagery of the poem's courtly surface.[1] Furthermore, the pun on "palace" ("paleys") and "Pallas" is a significant conflation of the two major divinities of the poem, the goddess of Troy and the goddess of Troilus; the images are brought together when Troilus refers to Criseyde's house as the "shryne, of which the seynt is oute!" (5.553). When Troilus stands before this palace, he recreates the opening episode of the poem, the feast honoring Pallas, at which he first saw his "saint" in her shrine.

Troilus recounts his new sorrows and old joys to Pandarus and rides "up and down" through Troy to recall the sites of his meetings with Criseyde. Once again he seems to see her in these familiar places (5.579) and finds so much stored in his memory that one could "a book make of it, lik a storie" (5.585). Pacing "up and down" at the gates of the city (5.605), Troilus fantasizes, seeing himself as disfigured: "And of hymself ymagened he ofte / To ben defet and pale" (5.617–18). Further references to storytelling suggest narrative self-consciousness; at this point the poem is a story about a man who makes up stories, a tale about telling tales. It is easy to see why Troilus needs to tell stories and why he believes in dreams. "When one understands a real event," according to Judson Boyce Allen, "it is because one has seen it in the shape of a literary event. The story of the past and the experience of the present really become true only as each rises to the character of what we would now call fiction."[2] Troilus gives the shape of literary events to the real events around him; he imagines that others, seeing him, expect him to die soon. In so doing, he uses the discourse of his sorrow, interior and secret, to inspire song, a form of "fiction" for his own consumption and his own consolation that he also imagines as public discourse, the subject of others' commentary.

The song of Troilus in book 5, a single stanza, recovers the nautical metaphors of the earlier books, identifying Criseyde as the "light" by which he steers, the source of his "gydyng" beams (5.638–44). He then turns to the source of other beams, to the

119

moon, whose horns dangerously signal cuckoldry: he says he will be glad when the moon has changed phases and is "horned newe," but the fact is that he will have been "horned," in effect made cuckold, by that time (5.650–51). Thus the narrator brings us to the ninth night of Troilus's vigil, when we return for the first time to Criseyde and the Greeks.

Criseyde laments Calkas's resistance to her suggestions about her departure. Unable to please him, she fears that, as her chances of success with her father lessen, Troilus will begin to doubt her. Her link between Troilus's views and her estimation of her own success is important, since her judgment becomes a self-fulfilling prophecy: the worse things appear for her among the Greeks, the more justified she is in thinking that Troilus has stopped believing in her. She fears that Troilus will think she is false, "and so it may wel seme," and then she will have "unthonk on every side" (5.698–99). By discounting the validity of all possible criticisms, she justifies the exercise of her own prerogatives. She sees no more alternatives among the Greeks than she had in Troy: if she tries to slip away she will either be apprehended as a spy or taken advantage of by some "wrecche," and in either case she is lost (5.701–7).

The narrator takes pains to attest to the sincerity of her grief and hopelessness; she has no one to complain to (5.727–28) and feels as excluded from Troy as Troilus feels deprived of her. Chaucer answers Troilus's contemplation of Criseyde's empty house with her contemplation of the city's walls and high towers. She briefly regrets that she did not run away with him (5.736–37), but then she recovers her wonted poise. Referring to "Prudence," who sees all with three eyes, Criseyde explains to herself that she could not see the trap that the future held: she could see the past plainly, and she could see the present, but no more (5.743–49). She renews her purpose to leave "to-morwe at nyght, by est or west" (5.751), as if direction were no consequence. There is a signal here for the reader. Criseyde's resolutions are always to take effect in the future that she cannot see, never in the present that she sees so clearly. At her conclusion the narrator says:

> But God it wot, er fully monthes two,
> She was ful fer fro that entencioun!
> For bothe Troilus and Troie town

Shal knotteles thorughout hire herte slide;
For she wol take a purpos for t'abide. (5.766–70)

The narrator then turns his attention to Diomede, who sets a
trap for Criseyde more like the manipulations of Pandarus than the
work of Troilus. Diomede observes that Criseyde never seems
happy—independent testimony to the sincerity of her love for
Troilus, perhaps? (5.780–82)—and takes this as confirmation that
she has a lover in Troy. Undaunted, he is guided by the proverbial
wisdom that Criseyde herself has spoken earlier: nothing ventured,
nothing gained (5.784; compare 2.807–8). Something of a scholar,
Diomede knows that "wise folk in bookes it expresse, / 'Men shal
nat wowe a wight in hevynesse' " (5.791). He is a better courtly lover
than Troilus in one important respect: unlike his Trojan counter-
part, Diomede both observes and reflects critically on the laws a
lover is expected to obey. He is also a practical man, noting that if
he fails he loses only his speech (5.798).

A strange disjunction follows: for the first time the narrator,
supplying framing details we might have expected in book 1, offers
physical descriptions of the major characters. Near the end of so
long a poem, the descriptions have the effect of an introduction and
recall Criseyde and Troilus before their misfortunes. At the same
time, one wonders why we find out now that Criseyde's brows were
"joyneden yfeere," her sole defect (joined eyebrows, 5.813), especially when the portraits of her two lovers are almost devoid of specific detail. Diomede merits a single stanza, Criseyde three, Troilus
two, and immediately following his description the narrator turns to
Diomede's conversation on the tenth and "fatal" day.

Diomede approaches Criseyde, first affecting to have some
business with Calkas (5.846–47). Diomede discusses the war and
makes touristlike small talk: does Criseyde find the Greeks and
their customs strange? (5.860–61). He also asks why she is not
married. Criseyde does not seem to suspect Diomede's intentions in
asking these questions, although the last of them would seem particularly pointed. He is encouraged by her response and asks if she
is unhappy because she has left a lover behind, adding, ominously,
that there is no point in longing for a Trojan, for Trojans are in
prison and none of them will survive the siege (5.877–89). The
Greeks will take such vengeance on Troy that thereafter no one will

again steal a queen as Paris stole Helen. Criseyde cannot have been reassured by his argument.

Calkas has foretold the city's fall "with ambages"—with ambiguities and "double wordes slye" (5.897–98)—but Diomede himself sees no ambiguity at all in the situation and demonstrates no doubts about himself. Criseyde can see for herself how matters lie. Calkas would not have proposed the exchange with Antenor if he was not sure that the city would be destroyed; that is why he wanted Criseyde out of Troy (5.904–910). Diomede urges her to "lat Troie and Troian fro youre herte pace!" (5.912). She can find, "er it be nyght" (5.919) a worthy Greek lover, better than any Trojan. Here Diomede fashions a becoming self for her benefit, blushing, and hesitating in his speech, a studied performance underscored by the narrator's multiple "Ands":

> And with that word he gan to waxen red,
> And in his speche a litel wight he quok,
> And caste asyde a litel wight his hed,
> And stynte a while; and afterward he wok,
> And sobreliche on hire he threw his lok,
> And seyde, "I am, al be it yow no joie,
> As gentil man as any wight in Troie." (5.925–31)

Diomede adds that, had his father Tideus lived (the king has been mentioned before, 5.88), he would have been a king himself; he asks for more time on the next day to explain himself, his delay until "to-morwe" supplying the perfect psychological gesture for a woman who has postponed all her major decisions in just the same way.

Criseyde grants his request, but the narrator finds it awkward to say so and reasserts her love for Troilus (5.953). She tells Diomede that she believes her father's prophecy, for he is "wys and redy" (5.964), but she adds that she loves her homeland and that Trojans are as worthy as people anywhere. Then, for the first time, she speaks of her first husband and, contradicting the narrator's claims about her fidelity, denies her lover's existence:

> I hadde a lord, to whom I wedded was,
> The whos myn herte al was, til that he deyde;

And other love, as help me now Pallas,
Ther in myn herte nys, ne nevere was. (5.975–78)

This sudden denial of Troilus cruelly contrasts with the narrator's claim that she had her "herte on Troilus / So faste that ther may it non arace" (5.953–54). Calling on Pallas again, she says that if she were to favor any of the Greeks, it would be Diomede; in any case, he may come again. She will not say "I will love you" or deny that she does; she will say only that she means well (5.1004). Greatly encouraged, as well he ought to be, Diomede takes her glove and leaves. Criseyde's speech to Diomede calls attention to the place of personal narrative and history in book 5. Just as, earlier, Troilus has told stories about himself and retold the history of their love (5.561–81), and as Cassandra will soon tell Troilus stories about the meaning of his dream, Criseyde here tells—reframes—the story of her life, substituting her first husband for Troilus and preparing herself for Diomede.

The structure of the narrative replays book 2, as though the story were fated to end in the shape of its beginning. In book 2 she saw Troilus from her window after hearing Pandarus extol the warrior's virtues; then she heard Antigone sing of love, slept, dreamed of the eagle, and began to favor Troilus. Now, following Diomede's visit, with the mediating, framing discourse of both the song and the dream replaced by the narrow boundaries of fate, she retires to consider his advantages. She needs friends but stands painfully alone; the contrast between the two situations is plainly obvious, and her decision to stay with the Greeks, where Diomede can protect her, suddenly seems an inevitable rather than a capricious choice. Thus, when Diomede comes the next day, all has been decided: "He refte hire of the grete of al hire peyne" (5.1036) and their affair begins. She gives him a steed that he once won from Troilus and gave to her; she also gives him a brooch that was Troilus's. "And that was litel nede," the narrator says (5.1040; see the brooch at 3.1370). When Diomede is injured in battle by Troilus, she heals him, just as she cured Troilus when he feigned illness at Deiphebus's house; the narrator adds, almost as an aside, that "she yaf hym hire herte" (5.1050). This, the narrator notes, is what the stories say, but he has also heard stories that tell of her woe at betraying Troilus. Criseyde contemplates the loss of her reputation:

Allas, of me, unto the worldes ende,
Shal neyther ben ywriten nor ysonge
No good word, for thise bokes wol me shende.
O, rolled shal I ben on many a tonge!
Thorughout the world my belle shal be ronge!
And wommen moost wol haten me of alle. (5.1058–63)

Little could either she or Chaucer have known how much would be said about her exactly as predicted here, once Robert Henryson and Renaissance balladeers took up Criseyde as a subject.

Criseyde correctly concludes that she has no options; her acts are fated and so is her resolution when she says, as a weary afterthought, "To Diomede algate I wol be trewe" (5.1071). Concerning Troilus she says (truthfully, to be sure) that she never wants to see him harmed; "al shal passe," she adds, echoing the wisdom of pragmatism that Pandarus has voiced (5.1085). Then the narrator issues a disclaimer: none of his sources actually say how long it was before she abandoned Troilus for Diomede, as if the duration of her fidelity were the major issue. He does not want to criticize her, for "hire name, allas, is publysshed so wide / That for hire gilt it oughte ynough suffise" (5.1095–96). In any case he excuses her "for she so sory was for hire untrouthe" (5.1098).

The resolution of the plot now fully revealed, the narrator returns for the last time to Troy. Criseyde's thoughts and actions will hereafter be represented in letters and in Troilus's memory. The narrator takes over for her, allowing her to speak only in absentia and allowing Troilus to dominate the rest of the action. Troilus continually thinks that he has seen her but looks at nothing (5.1120); he does not give up hope, and Pandarus allows him to be encouraged, although the narrator says that Fortune fools them both (5.1134). Troilus excuses her, blaming her father and even the porters who do not keep the gates open late enough (5.1140). Troilus thinks he has counted the days incorrectly (5.1185) but slowly faces the fact that she has broken her promise and is not returning. Finally he abandons hope and—characteristically —prepares for his death (5.1211). He is changed physically; both Priam and Troilus's mother ask why he is so sorrowful (we have to remember that they have no reason to suspect his affair). He says that he has "a grevous maladie / Aboute his herte" and that he is about to die (5.1231–32). He dreams again, this time a violently disturbing dream.

> He mette he saugh a bor with tuskes grete,
> That slepte ayeyn the bryghte sonnes hete.
> And by this bor, faste in his armes folde,
> Lay, kyssyng ay, his lady bryght, Criseyde. (5.1238–41)

This dream assures him of Criseyde's betrayal, and he renounces her. Pandarus reverts to his denunciation of dreams (5.1277–88) and says that the dream is actually about Criseyde and her father. He suggests that Troilus write a letter to find out for sure. If she is untrue, she will not reply; and if she does reply, then Troilus will know "as wheither she hath any liberte / To come ayeyn" (5.1299–1300). Over 100 lines long (5.1317–1421), Troilus's letter shows him, two months into their separation (5.1348), returned to his earlier self, restrained and courtly. The letter incorporates a number of familiar images and motifs, including the flight of the soul (5.1370); the contraries of joy and woe (5.1377); Criseyde's function as his guiding star (5.1392–93) and as his healer, or "whole-restorer" (5.1416–20).

The narrator merely paraphrases Criseyde's brief response, no doubt in an attempt to minimize her apparent duplicity. The reply is evasive: she "wolde come, and mende al that was mys," and "wolde come, ye, but she nyste whenne" (5.1426–28). She swears that she loves Troilus, but he finds her words "botmeles bihestes," empty promises (5.1431). Unconsoled, Troilus returns to meditate about his recent dream of the boor and calls his sister, Cassandra, to interpret it for him. With an extensive and pitiless analysis, she destroys the last illusions of hope that Troilus has entertained. She tells of the descent of Tideus, Diomede's father, and the saga of Thebes that Criseyde and her ladies were hearing when Pandarus appeared at the start of book 2 (Amphiorax is mentioned there and here, 5.1500). She concludes:

> This Diomede hire herte hath, and she his.
> Wep if thow wolt, or lef, for out of doute,
> This Diomede is inne, and thow art oute. (5.1517–19)

Troilus furiously rejects her word—who could believe Cassandra, after all?—and ridicules her analysis. Suddenly recovered, "as though al hool hym hadde ymad a leche" (5.1537), Troilus determines to investigate matters for himself. But just as he rises to his purpose, the fortunes of Troy begin to fall. Hector is killed (5.1548–50). The narrator says that everyone who "haunteth armes" ought to lament his death. Grieved at his brother's death, Troilus renews his hope for Criseyde's return, again blaming her father for her failure to come back (5.1574–75). Troilus writes many letters before Criseyde replies "for routhe" (for pity). Her concern with reputation is still prominent; but she will be able to put the rumors to rest "with dissymelyng" (5.1613). She will return, but the year or day remains uncertain (5.1619). Then she calls on his good faith. "For trewely, while that my lif may dure, / As for a frend ye may in me assure" (5.1623–24).

"A frend"? Troilus has the wit to see this letter as "a kalendes of chaunge" (5.1634), but he does not abandon hope until he sees the brooch he had given Criseyde on Diomede (5.1660–65). Her "name of trouthe / Is now fordon," he says, and this is just as the narrator had predicted (5.1686–87). Troilus blames Pandarus for criticizing the reliability of dreams and prepares to battle Diomede for revenge. Pandarus says nothing except, "I hate, ywys, Criseyde" (5.1732). He accuses her of treason and wishes for her death in a disturbing intersection of the poem's classical or pagan and Christian worlds: "And fro this world, almyghty God I preye / Delivere hire soon!" (5.1742–43). Pandarus has no more to say: this imprecation marks his final appearance. Reclaiming the mediator's role for himself, resuming his initial position as framer, and voicing the absolute powerlessness of humans confined by the frame of fate, the narrator echoes Pandarus:

> Swich is this world, whoso it kan byholde;
> In ech estat is litel hertes reste.
> God leve us for to take it for the beste! (5.1748–50)

The poem then turns to its first, and final, subject—its hero. Troilus dedicates himself to the war. He meets Diomede often in battle; they fight fiercely, but it is not Fortune's will that either kill the other (5.1763–64). The narrator once again backs away from the war story, however, saying that he will not write about "the armes of this ilke worthi man," or of "batailles," but of "his love" instead (5.1767–70). The echo of the *Aeneid* creates the first of the poem's many closing gestures or frames, a demarcation between the public subject of war and the private subject of love that allows the narrator to turn to his female audience.

The narrator offers a brief apology to women. Although Criseyde was untrue, he hopes that women will not hold it against him; indeed, he would gladly tell another story about Alceste or Penelope, and in *The Legend of Good Women* Chaucer turned to their stories in mock penance for having told the story of Criseyde's infidelity (5.1777–78). But with tongue already in cheek, the narrator turns his story of woman's infidelity around. He denounces the "false folk" who "with hire grete wit and subtilte" betray women, and then he warns, "Beth war of men, and herkneth what I seye!" (5.1781–85).

Often seen as farce and comedy, this absurd passage is not without effect in underscoring the parallels between the social worlds inside and outside of the poem. Criseyde has already reflected on women's powerlessness and expressed her fear that she will live in infamy because of her infidelity. The narrator seems at least partially earnest in adopting a perspective so similar to hers. Criseyde's conclusion about the whole episode might well be that all her troubles can be attributed to the interference of men— Troilus, Pandarus, and Diomede—in a life already complicated by her father's treason and her husband's death. Benson is right to identify this passage as rich in its appeals to different readers and their social and political interests.[3]

The appeal to the sympathy of "every gentil womman" is a second frame dividing the poem's male and female readers, a frame that is reversed, first used to isolate the guilty woman, Criseyde, and then turned so that all men, the "false folk," are made the subject instead. Then follows a rapid series of closing gestures, each of which frames a different aesthetic and ethical issue. These frames do the work of the introductions to the previous four books, but now the entire poem, not only book 5, is enclosed.

The next frame is the introduction of the envoi or palinode, "Go, litel bok, go, litel myn tragedye." The writer hopes that God will someday allow him, the book's "makere," to "make in som come-dye!" (5.1786–88). To emphasize the relation of this text to classical models and so to establish a historical perspective, the book is commended to Virgil, Ovid, Homer, Lucan, and Statius. These lofty precedents constitute a frame between the traditional and the new; this "litel bok" is to bridge the divide. Immediately thereafter the narrator turns to the present and, specifically, to the moment of writing. The immaturity of the English tradition causes the narrator to invoke the material process of reproducing his tale, the process of its history.

> And for ther is so gret diversite
> In Englissh and in writyng of oure tonge,
> So prey I God that non myswrite the,
> Ne the mysmetre for defaute of tonge;
> And red wherso thow be, or elles songe,
> That thow be understonde, God I bisechel
> But yet to purpos of my rather speche. (5.1793–99)

It is not too much to say that, in this busy sequence of changing frames, from genre to textual criticism, Chaucer's palinode anticipates almost all the issues that the critical tradition would ultimately address. Here we find revisionist thoughts about women; anxiety about accuracy in the textual tradition; nationalistic concern with language; obsessive competition with the classics; authorial anxiety about reputation and status; and more. What we do not find, and this can come as no surprise, is a concern with contemporary (that is, fourteenth-century) politics, a concern that Chaucer's readers, up to the late nineteenth century anyway, were happy to supply for themselves—a concern without which, it is safe to say, they would not have read his poetry.

The political content in *Troilus and Criseyde* is little more than a synonym for public life. War, as we have often been told, is not the chief concern. The narrator returns to war only to say that Troilus was without equal, except for Hector, and that Achilles killed Troilus, although we are given no details (5.1806). Troilus's death sets off a new series of frames. His spirit ascends to the eighth sphere from which he sees "erratik sterres, herkenyng armonye / With sownes ful of hevenyssh melodie" (5.1812–13). The perspective recalls the dreams of the poem and looks back to the major medieval source on dreams, *The Commentary on the Dream of*

Scipio by Macrobius. Chaucer also used this text in *The Parliament of Fowls*, in which he describes how the elder Scipio Africanus appeared to Scipio the Younger in a dream (185–129 B.C.), showing him Carthage and the Roman political world "from a sterry place" (43–49). This view is relevant to *Troilus and Criseyde*:

> Thanne shewede he hym the lytel erthe that here is,
> At regard of the hevenes quantite;
> And after shewede he hym the nyne speres;
> And after that the melodye herde he
> That cometh of thilke speres thryes thre,
> That welle is of musik and melodye
> In this world here, and cause of armonye.
> Than bad he hym, syn erthe was so lyte,
> And dissevable and ful of harde grace,
> That he ne shulde hym in the world delyte. (*PF*, 57–66)

With sounds of "hevenyssh melodie" in his ears, Troilus looks down at

> This litel spot of erthe that with the se
> Embraced is, and fully gan despise
> This wrecched world, and held al vanite
> To respect of the pleyn felicite
> That is in hevene above. (5.1815–19)

In book 1 Troilus fell in love; in book 3 he fell into place; in book 5 he fell out of love and hence out of place. Now, at the very end, he seems to rise to new heights. But is this a hero's reward for a life well led? His scorn for love, which was habitual until he loved and which resurfaced only when love abandoned him, is crassly convenient. It is no consolation to him; to us it seems little more than a bitter reflection on the possibilities of human happiness. "To practice this preachment," Richard Waswo writes, "would be paralysis: we would do no business, have no love affairs, and write no poems."[4] The hero has died for love and has been rewarded for his constancy, and although he laughs at those who mourn him and holds his own "werk" as "vanite," he judges his actions as foolish only when it is too late to retract them. To whom is this knowledge useful? Not to Troilus, certainly. Nor is it useful to Criseyde, who is stranded friendless in the middle of the war, in the power of two men—her father and her new lover—whose ambitions for her do not really differ from those proposed by her uncle and her previous lover.

Troilus is made to denounce "al oure werk" that follows "blynde lust" and cannot last when we should "al oure herte on heven caste." The narrator's Christian sentiments overtake the hero's voice when Troilus's laughter at the grief of his friends—an impressive detail—shrinks, midstanza, into a tired sigh of conventional piety. With this laughter Troilus turns his back on the world. He might as well leave, for the narrator has stopped listening to Troilus; the transmission from his satellite is intercepted, interrupted, and corrupted; his voice and view are lost. Troilus continues to the place "ther as Mercurye sorted hym to dwelle" (5.1827), an imprecise, vague location that does not seem to be a place of rest. But he remains in the eternal and unchanging world of harmony to which he has ascended, in the Boethian symbolic order, peaceful, perfect—and inhuman.

"Swich fyn hath, lo, this Troilus for love!" the narrator cries. But the reader might well reply that Troilus's parting thoughts were powerful and impressive. They held the imagination until the narrator spoiled them with an awkward infusion of piety whose only purpose is to prepare the way for a Christian denunciation of romantic love. His hero now protected from moral judgment, and his own judgment now stage center, the narrator excoriates the attachment that has brought Troilus such misery (5.1828–34). As an alternative to this tragic and waste of nobility and worthiness, the narrator proposes a comedy of Christian redemption. The "yonge, fresshe folkes, he or she" are exhorted:

> And of youre herte up casteth the visage
> To thilke God that after his ymage
> Yow made, and thynketh al nys but a faire,
> This world that passeth soone as floures faire. (5.1835–41)

This final recourse to natural cycles as an emblem of transitory happiness urges the audience to call on Christ's cross, for the God who sits "in hevene above" will be false to no one (presumably unlike Criseyde, Troilus's goddess). Troilus also sits in heaven above, of course, but the religion he espoused has now been banished, and with it both the ethical system to which it belonged—classical antiquity, the world of the gods—and its aesthetic response—tragedy. The pagan world retreats further as the narrator denounces "payens corsed olde rites" and the "rascaille" of the pagan gods.

The narrator directs those who want such stories to consult "the forme of olde clerkis speche / In poetrie, if ye hire bokes seche" (5.1854–55). He himself has a higher purpose: the dedication of the book to John Gower and Ralph Strode, to whom he sends it for "correction." This bow to contemporary philosophical authority is not gratuitous (although it verges on the obsequious). *Troilus and Criseyde* has earned its reputation as a philosophical work. Its Boethian thought is often only partially and inadequately understood by the characters, but Chaucer did not aim to produce a treatise; instead he wrote a poem of wisdom and folly about which many a treatise would come to be written. The narrator's final framing device is not this bid for recognition or the accompanying request for criticism from the wise. Rather it is a request for prayers from his readers, and with it we are back where we started. The narrator introduced the poem with a request for prayers; he concludes it with a prayer of his own ("I preye") that becomes our prayer too ("so make us"):

> And to that sothfast Crist, that starf on rode,
> With al myn herte of mercy evere I preye,
> And to the Lord right thus I speke and seye:
> Thow oon, and two, and thre, eterne on lyve,
> That regnest ay in thre, and two, and oon,
> Uncircumscript, and al maist circumscrive,
> Us from visible and invisible foon
> Defende, and to thy mercy, everichon,
> So make us, Jesus, for thi mercy, digne,
> For love of mayde and moder thyn benigne. Amen. (5.1860–69)

The prayer comes from Dante's *Paradiso* (14.28–30)[5]; it leaves behind not only the antique world of the love story and the epic but even the world in which this romance is being read.

Yet all this theology and prayer does not cancel out or even devalue the world Criseyde and Troilus have known. This long and moving poem about sexual love and social conflict frames our worlds and works unattractively only when our view of them no longer matters. Only when the relationship between the social world and its symbolic systems is reversed, so that symbolic overwhelms the social, can judgments so certain and negative as those of Troilus and the narrator be made. Only then can the claims of the social on the symbolic be abandoned. For Troilus, journeying among the spheres to which Mercury has guided him, and for the narrator, hovering in the sphere of Christian worship to which piety has guided him, only the symbolic is real. For the rest of us, the social is real, and as we stand amid the social world we feel—and we resist—the pull of symbolic systems created to tell us what the social should mean to us.

The narrator presumably returns from his religious trance, just as a priest does when his "Go, the Mass is ended" is followed by the noise of the congregation preparing to depart. Troilus is on the way to a resting place from which there is no return; he is, I think, lost in space. Criseyde too is lost in space, the undefined and largely undescribed world of the Greek camp that surrounds the city as if to frame it. Throughout the poem, the presence of the Greeks is visualized only vaguely; its power is registered instead through its effect on Troy and the Trojans, seen in their fear rather than seen in itself. Both Criseyde and Troilus are, in addition, lost in space of a different kind, the discursive space of the poem and its historical reception, a space readers share as they try to reconstruct both the woman and her desires and the man and his. The reader of *Troilus and Criseyde* who wants to know more about either Criseyde or Troilus can, finally, only reread the text. The dream-narrator of some of Chaucer's poems, including *The Book of the Duchess* and *The Parliament of Fowls*, returns to his books when he awakens from his vision. The reader of *Troilus and Criseyde* would do well to follow suit and to open another book, perhaps one of Chaucer's. My own impulse on reaching the end of *Troilus and Criseyde* is to go back to its beginning, where the narrator's prayer leads us. I find, no matter how often I reread the "olde clerkis speche," that the poem itself is always new.

10

Criseyde and Troilus

In 1896 T. R. Price analyzed the structure of *Troilus and Criseyde* to determine how the text was proportioned between direct and indirect discourse. He found that 64 percent was dialogue, 18 percent monologue, 14 percent group scenes, and 4 percent scenes involving three speakers.[1] The extraordinarily high proportion of dialogue and monologue is one reason why this poem is so difficult to follow: we hear characters' ideas directly and are left to interpret them as best we can, with assistance from a narrator who is sometimes confused himself. We know that in the Renaissance Chaucer's lovers were frequently portrayed in drama. For me the poem's extensive use of monologue and dialogue, and its lavish display of emotion, suggest opera as well. William Walton wrote an opera based on Shakespeare's play, but he was unhappy with Shakespeare's portrayal of Cressida. Through his librettist, Christopher Hassall, Walton discovered Chaucer's Criseyde, a portrayal which both Walton and Hassall found vastly more sympathetic.[2] But Walton's is not the opera that comes to my mind when I think about *Troilus and Criseyde*. Rather, I think of Richard Strauss's *Ariadne auf Naxos*.

This opera is not about a man and a woman but tells of two women, Ariadne (Chaucer wrote about her in *The Legend of Good Women*),[3] a Greek heroine of opera seria (tragedy), and Zerbinetta, a coquette who leads a commedia dell'arte troupe. Two troupes are scheduled to sing in separate entertainments, a tragedy and a bur-

133

lesque, to be performed on the same evening in the house of one of Vienna's wealthiest men. But time runs short, and just as the performance is about to begin the actors learn that the two halves of the program must be performed simultaneously. Thus Strauss's opera places tragic and comic figures on the same stage. Chaucer, in his conclusion to *Troilus and Criseyde*, likewise juxtaposes tragedy and comedy, and not only the Dantesque comedy of Christian redemption but a comedy of relief readers share with the characters. Chaucer creates a contrast between two ideas of love, the permanent and the changing, and seeks, in his final lines, to sweep the tension into a Christian doxology that supposedly neutralizes it. Not all readers wish to follow his edifying lead, however, and some may choose to linger over the poem's troubling but not unfamiliar split between the lover who believes in "the one and only" (Troilus) and the lover who cannot survive the sacrifice such lofty idealism demands (Criseyde).[4] This is a split also explored in Strauss's opera.

Ariadne has been abandoned by Theseus and languishes on a deserted island. She finds life without her "one and only" impossible: for her, it is either Theseus or death. When a ship approaches, she thinks Death's messenger has come for her: "Mutely my soul will follow its new lord, as a light leaf in the wind flutters downward, gladly falling." Zerbinetta marvels at Ariadne's solemnity and mocks her gloom. She says, "You do not wish to listen to me—beautiful and proud and still, like a statue on your own tomb." Zerbinetta believes in change. "Often when I believe I belong to one man alone, when I feel completely sure of myself, an as-yet-untasted freedom steals into my sweetly deluded heart." Whenever a new lover appears, he arrives like a god, and when he kisses her she "surrender[s] without a word." Later Zerbinetta comments, "Men! Dear God, if you really wanted us to resist them, then why did you create them all so different?"[5]

In this contrast between Ariadne, who cannot forget the one man she loved, and Zerbinetta, who can hardly remember all the men she has loved, we can (without being irreverent) see Troilus and Criseyde. He is the powerful, rigid, isolated idealist, obsessed with his desire for an unchanging world. She is the powerless pragmatist who must take circumstances, public or private, as they come. Troilus considers the ideology of the "one and only" sufficient; Criseyde knows that such an ideology would doom her to a world as bleak as Ariadne's, a prospect the Trojan woman rejects. Why can she not accept that prospect? Why can Troilus not accept life without her? Readers of *Troilus and Criseyde* puzzle about these questions after all others have been set aside. These are not questions that can be answered easily (or at all), but readers who are interested in love, idealism, and the limits of exclusivity, and who are challenged to undertake further work on this poem, can take up other issues. I would like to discuss two.

The first concerns Criseyde. A great deal has been written recently about her status as a woman. Much of this reconsideration is long overdue, but too much of it concerns the drama of her character and too little of it concerns her link to symbolic and social systems such as those I have discussed. Monica McAlpine has defended Criseyde as a woman "divested, by virtue of other peoples' choices, of all her worldly securities."[6] This is an important point, not because it is necessarily true (I would dispute it) but because it raises a more important point about the connection of words to things, of freedom to possessions, of independence to social status. Criseyde is not really divested of "all her worldly securities" by the choices of others. Indeed, she takes many such securities with her to the Greeks (see 4.1380–89). She is not deprived of things but rather of both her own choices and the opportunity to express them. Her second dream in book 2, for example, in which an eagle exchanges hearts with her, does not divest her of choices but creates choices that Chaucer ignores. What is remarkable about her long and forceful discussion with Troilus in book 4 is that Chaucer allows it to happen—allows us to know what she thinks. David Aers believes that at this point Criseyde endorses the male-dominated ideology of Troy as the right one.[7] What I think is that at this point, in comparison to other points, Chaucer shows her thinking and speaking for herself. He rarely does so; in fact, Chaucer's success in suppressing Criseyde's discourse has led many critics to see her as coy, mysterious, and "feminine."[8] But all she may be is silenced. Her value in the poem is not what she *says* to others but what she *stands for* in their eyes—what these others decide she may represent. Her importance is not that she *is* for herself but that she *signifies* for others who can make use of the symbolic value they assign to her.

Criseyde is a textbook illustration of Luce Irigaray's thesis about the relation of woman's pleasure to material circumstances. Earlier, I quoted Irigaray's view that "woman is never anything but the locus of a more or less competitive exchange between two men, including the competition for the possession of mother earth."9 We see in this poem that Criseyde stands between two men, Troilus and Pandarus, who are not in competition but whose homosocial bond necessitates her mediation. The pleasure of their companion-ship seems to require her existence. Certainly their friendship flourishes because of her, in part because Pandarus seems to find expression for his sexuality through Troilus's passion for her; and perhaps Pandarus's bitter denunciation of her betrayal reflects an end to the intimate bond he has formed with the hero.

In order to fulfill this role in the larger symbolic system or in this smaller, more intimate version of a man-to-man relationship, in order to supply a locus for others and their discourse, a woman cannot have value in or of herself. Rather, Irigaray says, she must be the bearer of value for others, of exchange value, so that she can "put men into touch with each other" and "assure the possibility of the use and circulation of the symbolic without being [a recipient] of it." Woman's pleasure threatens the symbolic order of courtly love, which exists to gratify the male's sexuality and aggression in the guise of gentle conduct; preservation of that order requires that her pleasure be suppressed. Irigaray adds that women's "nonaccess to the symbolic [order] is what has established the social order" (Irigaray, 189–90). Criseyde's "nonaccess" to the symbolic order is ensured by her exclusion from many kinds of discourse in the poem. At the same time, her exchange value maintains the social order of Troy, at least temporarily, and the homosocial intimacy of Pandarus and Troilus. This is the use that the poem makes of her. The price of her participation in the symbolic order, demonstrated by her function in the social order, is her silence.

Irigaray argues that whatever gives pleasure to women without also giving pleasure to the men around them is forbidden. Women have only extrinsic rather than intrinsic value; they have value only to give to others. Considering this point, we can understand the bleak scene in book 4 in which Criseyde is surrounded by admiring ladies who expect her to be happy that she will rejoin her father. No one in this dreary group can tell us what Criseyde really stands for, what she is worth. For only women are present, and to them Criseyde has value only in the eyes of her father (they do not know about her affair with Troilus, or they would understand her unhappiness). Thus they expect her to be pleased that she will soon rejoin her father, a—*the?*—man to whom she means something. Rejoin her father? How can this be a woman's idea of womanly happiness? It can be an ideal only for women who have no value in themselves and who look outside themselves, to men, for value.

Criseyde remains an empty vehicle, waiting to take on the value that others give her. When, in rapid succession, she proves valuable to her father, to Hector, to the parliament, and to the citizens of Troy, she is not much different from the statue of Pallas Athena, for she is nearly as deprived of independent motion and speech as a block of marble. Would Zerbinetta, beholding Criseyde, think of her as another Ariadne, as mute as a statue on her own tomb? The coquette would probably consider Criseyde, who in her Chaucerian guise (if not in later manifestations) wants only to replace one true love with another, as something of an idealist. That generations of writers after Chaucer have vilified Criseyde as a whore and a slut is a nasty tribute to the power of imagination to find corruption wherever it must and to fit Criseyde's circumstances into a rigid, moralistic framework. Zerbinetta, I believe, would know better.

We, of course, know that it is Troilus, not Criseyde, who thinks about his tomb, although to think of a hero so voluble and so in motion (so in emotion) as a mute statue is not easy. So, finally, I re-examine Troilus, again with Irigaray's help. "Masculine language," she writes, "is not understood with any precision. . . . So long as men claim to say everything and define everything, how can anyone know what the language of the male sex might be? So long as the logic of discourse is modeled on sexual indifference, on the submission of one sex to the other, how can anything be known about the 'masculine'?" (Irigaray, 128). Here, I think, is a point Chaucerians have just begun to consider. What a wealth of things there are to be said about women in literature! Women are constantly discussed by critics manifesting the enthusiasm of explorers who have just discovered a new continent. Rushing to join this discussion, Chaucerians have mistakenly assumed that everything about men has already been said. It has not. When Chaucerians—

137

guilty liberals, many of them, eager to find in Chaucer another guilty liberal like themselves—begin to take gender seriously, as meaning more than championing oppressed women, they will begin to listen to Chaucer's men with equal attentiveness. What has already been said has, for the most part, been said by men who have been assumed to be speaking for women as well as for themselves. This assumption forgets that, in literature as in life, men may often be more powerful than women but that they participate in a single system more powerful than either sex and not in the power of either sex.

But when I consider what this system is, I find that I confront a universal claim with a rather short history. Judith Butler has recently challenged the "universal logic" behind the much-discussed system of exchange that Claude Lévi-Strauss proposed as the basis of all kinship structures. Butler elaborates the importance of the challenge to that universal claim in Irigaray's view that the "reciprocal exchange between men presupposes a nonreciprocity between the sexes." The exchange bonds men, as it does Pandarus and Troilus, as it does (temporarily at least) the states of Greece and Troy. But is bonding between women also possible? Irigaray asserts that "the labor force and its products . . . are the object of transactions among men and men alone. This means that the *very possibility of a sociocultural order requires homosexuality* as its organizing principle" (Irigaray, 192–93). Butler points out that such a system effectively excludes the possibility of a female or lesbian "economy," simply refuses to consider the possibility because Lévi-Strauss did not raise it.[10] When that possibility is raised, homosocial bonding will no longer involve men alone. And when that happens, we can begin to consider what men have to say for themselves—what Troilus has to say for himself, and to other men. That speech remains to be heard. But first it must be thought.

How do we find out what men think and how they speak? In her discussion of Chaucer's "sexual poetics" Carolyn Dinshaw claims that Troilus, Pandarus, and the narrator (not to mention certain famous Chaucerians) "all read like men: they invoke structures of authority in order to order the disorder, to stop the restless desire represented in and enacted by their texts, to find rest." She continues, "Everyone needs such rest, of course, not just men."[11] Dinshaw is attempting to find out what it means to "read like a woman," and in so doing posits shifts in the positions men and women can occupy as they read. Some of Chaucer's men, she shows, can read as women do; Troilus is certainly one of them. Aers, we have seen, also thinks that Criseyde reads (or at least thinks) like a man. Both scholars—whose work I consider among the very best available to students of Chaucer—help us consider Irigaray's point that "language" and "masculine language" should not be confused. "Masculine language" is what men say *as men*, not as men speaking for women. Which men do not speak for women? Troilus is one, I think. We see in book 3 that he can take the woman's part in the "dawn song," and we have many other signs that he is not afraid of the emotional displays that Pandarus, Troilus's first and therefore model "reader," finds so embarrassing. Troilus is many men; he is also many women. Which one does he read like? Must he read only like one or the other? If we read Troilus like a man, we box him into Dinshaw's structures of authority. If we read Troilus in other ways—if we look at him at the end of the poem—we know that his rest in the spheres is only temporary. Troilus remains in motion, lost in space, traveling among those structures of authority, not at home among them.

At the end of *Ariadne auf Naxos*, Ariadne and Bacchus are both transformed, Ariadne into a constellation, Bacchus into the god he did not know he was. Zerbinetta gazes at their rapture and smiles to see her tragic rival, as if following the coquette's advice, taking a new lover after all. It is Troilus who is transformed at the end of *Troilus and Criseyde*, but of course it is Criseyde who, from the first, became the star. His value seems self-evident and self-expressed, while her value must be constructed because her speech tells us so little. We cannot make up Criseyde's thoughts, surely, but we should look more closely at the acts and signs that the text substitutes for her spoken discourse. And we can surely make more of the thoughts of Troilus, whose language has yet to be understood as man's language.

Chaucerians who contemplate the end of the poem will not cease to muse on its ironies. And in those musings we can take hope. For the ending is a frame, but just one frame of many that Chaucer constructed and that his readers continue to reconstruct. I am aware, at the end of this introduction to the poem, that I have also introduced the frame as a critical concept without exploring its riches. The many possibilities that the frame creates are, I realize, only sampled on the discussions of each book that follow my fourth chapter. But if frames have to be drawn for us—and drawn they are, by our academic calendar, and by the requirements of our publishers—no frame is final, including the framework of this study. There are other studies of the frame, and of this poem, and more will follow this one. And why not? After all these books, all these articles, all these papers, notes, and speeches—after all these frames—there will be, it is good to think, still more to say.

notes and references

Chapter 1

1. For "Lak of Stedfastnesse" (26–28), see Benson, *The Riverside Chaucer*, 654; hereafter cited in text as *RC*.

2. May McKisack, *The Fourteenth Century, 1307–1399* (Oxford: Clarendon Press, 1959), xvii.

3. J. D. Maddicott, "The English Peasantry and the Demands of the Crown, 1294–1341," in *Landlords, Peasants, and Politics in Medieval England*, ed. T. H. Aston (Cambridge: Cambridge University Press, 1987), 285–359.

4. See Christopher Dyer, "The Social and Economic Background to the Rural Revolt of 1381," 9–42, and A. F. Butcher, "English Urban Society and the Revolt of 1381," 84–111, in *The English Rising of 1381*, ed. R. H. Hilton and T. H. Aston (Cambridge: Cambridge University Press, 1984).

5. This summary draws on the introduction by Martin M. Crow and Virginia E. Leland in Benson, *RC*, xviii–xxvi.

6. Strohm, *Social Chaucer*, x; on idealization, see 107.

7. Anne Middleton, "The Idea of Public Poetry in the Reign of Richard II"; see also Middleton, "Chaucer's 'New Men' and the Good Literature of *The Canterbury Tales*," in *Literature and Society*, ed. Edward W. Said (Baltimore: Johns Hopkins University Press, 1980), 15–56.

8. Larry D. Benson, "The Occasion of *The Parliament of Fowls*," in *The Wisdom of Poetry: Essays in Early English Medieval Culture in Honor of Morton W. Bloomfield*, ed. Larry D. Benson and Siegfried Wenzel (Kalamazoo, Mich.: Medieval Institute, 1982), 123–44.

9. Quoted in translation from *The Major Latin Works of John Gower*, trans. Eric W. Stockton (Seattle: University of Washington Press, 1962), book 1, chap. 13, pp. 71–72.

10. On the possibility that "The Knight's Tale" refers to the rising as the "cherles rebellyng" Saturn claims to inspire (I.2459), see notes by Vincent J. DiMarco to this line (Benson, *RC*, 838).

11. J. Wright Duff, *A Literary History of Rome: From the Origins to the Close of the Golden Age*, cor. and ed. A. M. Duff (New York: Barnes & Noble, 1959), 256–57.

12. See David Aers, "*The Parliament of Foules*: Authority, the Knower, and the Known," *Chaucer Review* 16 (1981): 1–17.

13. Janet Coleman, "English Culture in the Fourteenth Century," in *Chaucer and the Italian Trecento*, ed. Piero Boitani (Cambridge: Cambridge University Press, 1983), 33–63; see esp. 59.

14. McKisack, *The Fourteenth Century*, 477, n. 2.

15. Pope, *How to Study Chaucer*, 6–8.

16. For *Mac Flecknoe* and *The Rape of the Lock*, see *The Norton Anthology of English Literature*, vol. 1, 5th ed., ed. M. H. Abrams et al. (New York: W. W. Norton, 1986), 1818–24, 2233–52.

Chapter 2

1. On the problems of Chaucer translations, see Peter G. Beidler, "Chaucer and the Trots: What to Do about Those Modern English Translations," *Chaucer Review* 19 (1985): 290–301. He discusses 10 translations but only one of *Troilus and Criseyde* (292, 299). I recommend the translation of this poem by Nevill Coghill, *Troilus and Criseyde* (New York: Penguin, 1971).

2. David Williams, "*The Canterbury Tales*": *A Literary Pilgrimage* (Boston: G. K. Hall, 1987), 8.

3. Spurgeon, for example, in *Five Hundred Years of Chaucer Criticism*, calls the poem "the first great tragic novel" (1:lxxvii).

Chapter 3

1. Alice Kaminsky surveys modern criticism in *Chaucer's "Troilus and Criseyde" and the Critics* (Athens: Ohio University Press, 1980). Reservations about her work are found in David Staines's review, *Speculum* 57 (1982): 351–53. Good bibliographical guides include Boitani and Mann, *The Cambridge Chaucer Companion*, 243–54, and John Leyerle and Anne Quick, *Chaucer: Bibliographical Introduction* (Toronto: University of Toronto Press, 1986).

2. On the manuscript tradition, see comments by Stephen A. Barney in Benson, *RC*, 1161–62.

3. See Spurgeon, *Five Hundred Years of Chaucer Criticism*, 1:x–xi. For additions to Spurgeon's lists, see Hyder E. Rollins, "The Troilus-Criseyde Story from Chaucer to Shakespeare," *PMLA* 32 (1917): 383–429.

4. Windeatt, *Chaucer's "Troilus and Crisyede."* Some of the information in the edition is also available in Windeatt's study, "The Scribes as Chaucer's Early Critics," *Studies in the Age of Chaucer* 1 (1979): 119–41.

5. In Ruggiers, *Editing Chaucer*, see Beverly Boyd, "William Caxton," 13–34, and James E. Blodgett, "William Thynne," 35–52. On the nature of Pynson's additions, see Blodgett, 41–43.

6. In Ruggiers, *Editing Chaucer*, see Blodgett, 35–52.

7. Root, *The Book of Troilus and Criseyde*, lxiv.

8. Henryson, *The Testament of Cresseid*, 9, 19.

Notes and References

9. In Ruggiers, *Editing Chaucer*, see Blodgett, 50.

10. In Ruggiers, *Editing Chaucer*, see Anne Hudson, "John Stow," 53–70, esp. 53–54.

11. In Ruggiers, *Editing Chaucer*, see Blodgett, 38–39.

12. On Foxe, Bale, and Parker, see Allen J. Frantzen, *Desire for Origins: New Language, Old English, and Teaching the Tradition* (New Brunswick, N.J.: Rutgers University Press, 1990).

13. In Ruggiers, *Editing Chaucer*, see Derek Pearsall, "Thomas Speght," 88.

14. Because of their reputation as sympathizers, Chaucer and Gower were excepted from the early authors denounced in the Act of Advancement of True Religion in 1570. See Spurgeon, *Five Hundred Years of Chaucer Criticism*, 1:105–6; quote from Foxe is from p. 106.

15. In Ruggiers, *Editing Chaucer*, see Pearsall, 75–80.

16. Henryson, *The Testament of Cresseid*, 19; in Ruggiers, *Editing Chaucer*, Pearsall, 71–92; see esp. 86–88. On Speght, see also Johan Kerling, *Chaucer in Early English Dictionaries* (Leiden: Leiden University Press, 1979; The Hague: Martinus Nijhoff, 1979).

17. On Speght's defense of Chaucer's meter, in Ruggiers, *Editing Chaucer*, see Pearsall, 86; on Pearsall's view of the decline of Chaucer's reputation, see 91.

18. The *Preface to Fables Ancient and Modern* is quoted from Abrams et al., *Norton Anthology*, 1850–51.

19. Root, *The Book of Troilus and Criseyde*, lxvii.

20. Francis Kinaston, writing in 1635, was apparently the first to state that the *Testament* was not Chaucer's. In Ruggiers, *Editing Chaucer*, see William L. Alderson, "John Urry," 108; but see also Henryson, *The Testament of Cresseid*, 19.

21. Some of the illustrations in Urry's edition are reproduced in Betsy Bowden, *Chaucer Aloud* (Philadelphia: University of Pennsylvania Press, 1987). The copy of Urry's edition in the Folger Library, Washington, D.C., contains portraits of Urry (the frontispiece) and Chaucer (opposite the "Life of Chaucer").

22. In Ruggiers, *Editing Chaucer*, Barry A. Windeatt, "Thomas Tyrwhitt," 117–43; see esp. 118.

23. Root, *The Book of Troilus and Criseyde*, lxvii–lxviii.

24. For editions after Bell, see Root, *The Book of Troilus and Criseyde*, lxix–lxx, and Spurgeon, *Five Hundred Years of Chaucer Criticism*, 1:lxx–lxxii.

25. On the work of the New Chaucer Society, see Paul G. Ruggiers, "The Variorum Chaucer," *Chaucer Newsletter* 1 (1979): 24–26.

26. Root, *The Book of Troilus and Criseyde*, lii.

27. H. Bergen, ed., *Lydgate's Troy Book*, Early English Text Society, ES 97, 103, 106, 126 (London: Oxford University Press, 1906–35; reprint, New York: Kraus, 1973). See C. David Benson, *The History of Troy in Middle English Literature* (Woodbridge, Suffolk: D. S. Brewer, 1980), 97–129.

28. Denton Fox, "The Scottish Chaucerians," in *Chaucer and Chauceri-ans*, ed. D. S. Brewer (University, Ala.: University of Alabama Press, 1966), 164–200.

29. See Rollins, "The Troilus-Criseyde Story," 396. The standard edition of the poem is edited by Denton Fox.

30. Skelton's poem is found in *Tottel's Miscellany* of 1557; see Spurgeon, *Five Hundred Years of Chaucer Criticism*, 1:68.

31. In Ruggiers, *Editing Chaucer*, see Blodgett, 38–39. See also Veré Laurel Rubel, *Poetic Diction of the English Renaissance* (New York: Modern Language Association, 1941), 14–30, and Raymond Southall, *The Courtly Maker: An Essay on the Poetry of Wyatt and His Contemporaries* (Oxford: Basil Blackwell, 1964), 11–14, 35–39.

32. In Rubel, *Poetic Diction*, 23–28. See also Herbert G. Wright, *A Seven-teenth-Century Modernization of the First Three Books of Chaucer's "Troilus and Criseyde"* (Berne: Francke Verlag, 1960), 9; quotation from Spurgeon, *Five Hundred Years of Chaucer Criticism*, 1:126.

33. Lee Patterson, "Ambiguity and Interpretation: A Fifteenth-Century Reading of *Troilus and Criseyde*," in *Negotiating the Past: The Historical Un-derstanding of Medieval Literature* (Madison: University of Wisconsin Press, 1987), 115–53; see esp. 124 and 148–49.

34. Sidnam's text is quoted from Wright, *A Seventeenth-Century Mod-ernization*, 75–78, 80.

35. James Russell Lowell, "Chaucer," *North American Review* 111 (1870): 155–98. Quoted in Spurgeon, *Five Hundred Years of Chaucer Criticism*, 2:108.

36. See D. W. Robertson, Jr., *A Preface to Chaucer* (Princeton, N.J.: Princeton University Press, 1962), for the foundational patristic reading of *Troilus and Criseyde*.

37. For a description of the division between medieval and Renaissance, see David Wallace, "Carving Up Time and the World: Medieval-Renaissance Turf Wars; Historiography and Personal History," Working Paper No. 11 (Milwaukee: University of Wisconsin, Center for Twentieth-Century Studies, 1990–91).

Chapter 4

1. Benson, *Chaucer's "Troilus and Criseyde*," 60–61.

2. There is a good discussion of the contrast between mimetic and alle-gorical modes in Robert Kellogg and Oliver Steele, *The Faerie Queene: Books I and II, the Mutability Cantos, and Selections from the Minor Poetry* (Indianapolis: Bobbs-Merrill, 1965), 6–10. For a discussion of autobio-graphical and allegorical modes in the analysis of Chaucer's Pardoner, see Pearsall, *The Canterbury Tales*, 94–95.

3. Patterson, *Chaucer and the Subject of History*, 3, 5.

Notes and References

4. H. Marshall Leicester, Jr., *The Disenchanted Self: Representing the Subject in the Canterbury Tales* (Berkeley: University of California Press, 1990), 10, 14.

5. Ibid., 308; see also 21–26.

6. A standard discussion of character and subjectivity is David Carroll, *The Subject in Question: The Languages of Theory and the Strategies of Fiction* (Chicago: University of Chicago Press, 1982). Patterson, *Chaucer and the Subject of History*, and Leicester, *The Disenchanted Self*, both supply extended, specialized discussions of subjectivity in Chaucer's works.

7. John Frow, *Marxism and Literary History* (Oxford: Basil Blackwell, 1986), 220–21. Frow's discussion is based on Jacques Derrida, "The Parergon," *October* 9 (1979): 3–40. For a recent brief discussion, see Peter W. Travis, "Deconstructing Chaucer's Retraction," *Exemplaria* 3 (1991): 135–58; see esp. pp. 135–37.

8. Beidler, "Chaucer and the Trots," surveys the attempts of translators to obscure some of Chaucer's sexual humor. In *Chaucer's Bawdy* (New York: E. P. Dutton & Co., 1972), Thomas W. Ross surveys the poet's use of risqué terms and discusses scholarly evasions of them; see esp. 7–15.

9. The frame has long been a commonplace in criticism of the *Tales*. See Robert Armstrong Pratt and Karl Young, "The Literary Framework of *The Canterbury Tales*," in *Sources and Analogues of Chaucer's "Canterbury Tales*," ed. W. F. Bryan and Germaine Dempster (New York: Humanities Press, 1941), 1–81.

10. See Monica McAlpine, *The Genre of "Troilus and Criseyde*," for further discussion, and esp. 74–75 on "Boethian comedy."

11. This definition is adapted from Edward W. Said, *The World, the Text, and the Critic* (Cambridge: Harvard University Press, 1983), 47–49, a difficult but valuable discussion of criticism and its operations.

12. Shoaf, *Troilus and Criseyde*, xxii–xxiii.

13. This is done with irony in "The Clerk's Tale," for example, but the ballad I quote in the previous chapter, "Lak of Stedfastnesse," conveys the sentiment well: in previous ages, people behaved better.

14. Claude Lévi-Strauss, *The Elementary Structures of Kinship* (Boston: Beacon Press, 1969), 115; an important commentary is Gayle Rubin, "The Traffic in Women: Notes toward a Political Economy of Sex," in *Toward an Anthropology of Women*, ed. Rayna Reiter (New York: Monthly Review Press, 1975), 157–210.

15. Luce Irigaray, *This Sex Which Is Not One*, trans. Catherine Porter, with Carolyn Burke (Ithaca, N. Y.: Cornell University Press, 1985), 31–32. See also the discussion by Dinshaw, *Chaucer's Sexual Poetics*, 56–64, for a particularly useful analysis of the exchanges in this poem.

16. For a seminal discussion of this important model, see Georges Duby, *The Three Orders: Feudal Society Imagined*, trans. Arthur Goldhammer (Chicago: University of Chicago Press, 1980). On military violence, see 40–41 and 56–58.

17. Ibid., 105 (the three-legged stool) and 264–66 (the body).

18. Ibid., 110; on the power of symbolic systems to rationalize inequality, see Duby's comments, 115.

19. J. G. A. Pocock, "Texts as Events: Reflections on the History of Political Thought," in *The Politics of Discourse: The Literature and History of Seventeenth-Century England*, ed. Kevin Sharpe and Steven N. Zwicker (Berkeley: University of California Press, 1987), 21–34; see esp. 22–24.

20. Leicester, *The Disenchanted Self*, 8.

21. See Jordan, *Chaucer and the Shape of Creation*, for an elaborate discussion of the architectural features of the poem.

22. Frow, *Marxism and Literary History*, 224, quoting Lesley Stern, "Fiction/Film/Femininity I," *Australian Journal of Screen Theory*, 9–10 (1981): 39; see Frow, 265, n. 22.

Chapter 5

1. All quotations from *Troilus and Criseyde* are from Benson, *RC*, and are given by book and line number (e.g., 1.22 for book 1, line 22).

2. Benson, *Chaucer's "Troilus and Crideyde,"* 60–83. See also Patterson, *Chaucer and the Subject of History*, 92–99, on the meaning of Troy in Chaucer's idea of history.

3. See Wallace, "Continental Inheritance," in Boitani and Mann, *The Cambridge Chaucer Companion*, 19–37, and Winthrop Wetherbee, *Chaucer and the Poets*, for a wider discussion of Chaucer and Dante.

4. For a convenient collection of various sources, see *The Story of Troilus*, trans. R. K. Gordon (New York: E. P. Dutton & Co., 1964; reprint, Toronto: University of Toronto Press, 1979).

5. Richard Rambuss, " 'Processe of Tyme': History, Consolation, and Apocalypse in *The Book of the Duchess*," *Exemplaria* 2 (1990): 659–83; see esp. 673.

6. Aers, *Chaucer, Langland*, 117–42; see esp. 118–19.

7. See comments by Stephen Barney on 1.162–315 in Benson, *RC*, 1026. (Barney supplied the explanatory notes to the text.)

8. See Barney's note to 1.400–20 in Benson, *RC*, 1028.

9. The nautical metaphors in the poem are discussed by Stevens, "The Winds," 285–307.

10. Boethius, book 1, prose 4.2–3; all references are to the translation by Richard Green and hereafter are given in the text with citation of book and chapter (the latter designated as prose or poem).

11. In the *Parliament*, 11.415–41; "The Knight's Tale" is in Benson, *RC*, 37–66.

12. On homosocial bonding, see Eve Kosofsky Sedgwick, *Between Men: English Literature and Male Homosocial Desire* (New York: Columbia University Press, 1985), 1–48, where she discusses such bonds and homosexual relationships in the Renaissance.

Notes and References

Chapter 6

1. Diamond, "Troilus and Criseyde," 93.
2. See the list of these "rules" in Shoaf, *Troilus and Criseyde*, xxiv–xxv.
3. This is also the date of Palamon's escape from prison in "The Knight's Tale" (see I, 56); see Barney's note to the tale in Benson, *RC*, 1031.
4. Benson, *Chaucer's "Troilus and Criseyde,"* 66. Chaucer tells the legend of Philomela in *The Legend of Good Women* (Benson, *RC*, 624–26).
5. See Jill Mann, *Chaucer and Medieval Estates Satire* (Cambridge: Cambridge University Press, 1973), 257–58.
6. See Barney's notes to 2.507–53 in Benson, *RC*, 1033.
7. See Sister Mary Charlotte Borthwick, "Antigone's Song as 'Mirour' in Chaucer's 'Troilus and Criseyde,' " *Modern Language Quarterly* 22 (1961): 227–35.
8. I am among them. See my essay, "The 'Joie and Tene' of Dreams in *Troilus and Criseyde*," in *Chaucer in the Eighties*, ed. Julian N. Wasserman and Robert J. Blanch (Syracuse, N.Y.: Syracuse University Press, 1986), 105–19.
9. On these personifications, see Barney's comments on 2.1376 in Benson, *RC*, 1036.

Chapter 7

1. Elizabeth Salter, "*Troilus and Criseyde*: A Reconsideration," in *Patterns in Love and Courtesy: Essays in Memory of C. S. Lewis*, ed. John Lawler (London: Edward Arnold, 1966), 86–106; quotation from 103–4.
2. See Benson, *RC*, 1038, note to 3.273, for this explanation.
3. This speech, rather scholastic in nature, is incorrectly attributed to Pandarus in Benson, *RC*, 1039, note to 3.404; see Root's note to the same line in his edition.
4. Dinshaw, *Chaucer's Sexual Poetics*, 60–61.
5. See V. A. Kolve, "Chaucer's *Second Nun's Tale* and the Iconography of Saint Cecilia," in *New Perspectives in Chaucer Criticism*, ed. Donald M. Rose (Norman, Okla.: Pilgrim Press, 1981), 137–74.
6. See Root, *The Book of Troilus and Criseyde*, xvi–xviii, concerning the relevance of this conjunction to the 1385 date given for the poem.
7. See Barney's comments in Benson, *RC*, 1041, in the note to 3.813–33.
8. On the sexual meaning of the ring as an image of the pudendum, see Ross, *Chaucer's Bawdy*, 195–98.
9. On "dulcarnoun," which appears at what some take to be the mathematical center of the poem, see Barney's note in Benson, *RC*, 1041, to 3.931.
10. See R. E. Kaske, "The Aube in Chaucer's *Troilus*," in *Chaucer Criticism: "Troilus and Criseyde" and the Minor Poems*, ed. Richard J. Schoeck

and Jerome Taylor (Notre Dame: University of Notre Dame Press, 1961), 167–79; see Barney's note to 3.1422–1533 in Benson, *RC*, 1043.

11. Aers, *Chaucer, Langland*, 118–19 and elsewhere.

12. The "suggestiveness" of this scene has aroused interest in some feminist quarters of late; Barney's comments in Benson, *RC*, 1043, vigorously dismiss such readings.

13. See Barney's notes on the sources of these lines in Benson, *RC*, 1043.

Chapter 8

1. See Barney's note to 4.120–26 in Benson, *RC*, 1045, concerning Chaucer's sources.

2. Scholars once believed that Chaucer added this speech in revision, since some manuscripts contain it and others do not; current opinion has attributed this variation to scribal preference (with some scribes simply choosing to omit it) rather than to Chaucer's own design. I discuss this problem in chapter 3.

3. See John Huber, "Troilus' Predestination Soliloquy: Chaucer's Changes from Boethius," *Neuphilologische Mitteilungen* 66 (1965): 120–25.

4. Aers, *Chaucer, Langland*, 133. I am, in the main, sympathetic to Aers's portrayal of Criseyde.

Chapter 9

1. On "queynt," which means "pudendum" as well as "curious," see Ross, *Chaucer's Bawdy*, 174–84.

2. Judson Boyce Allen, *The Ethical Poetic of the Later Middle Ages* (Toronto: University of Toronto Press, 1982), 261. His remarks refer to the medieval audience's "willingness to blur the distinction between fact and false, and to receive stories as true more on the basis of their significance and their shape than their verifiability" (260).

3. Benson, *Chaucer's "Troilus and Criseyde,"* 50–52.

4. Richard Waswo, "The Narrator of *Troilus and Criseyde*," *English Literary History* 50 (1983): 1–25. This passage is quoted in Dinshaw, *Chaucer's Sexual Poetics*, 52.

5. On Chaucer's debt to Dante at this and other points, see Wetherbee, *Chaucer and the Poets*; on the conclusion, see 224–43.

Chapter 10

1. T. R. Price, "A Study in Chaucer's Method of Narrative Construction," *PMLA* 2 (1896): 307–22. Price's work is discussed in John North-Smith, *Geoffrey Chaucer* (London: Routledge & Kegan Paul, 1974), 172–73.

2. Gillian Widdicombe, "Troilus and Criseyde," commentary for the recording of William Walton, *Troilus and Cressida*, conducted by Lawrence Foster (London: EMI Records, 1977), 5–6.

3. "The Legend of Ariadne" is part 6 of *The Legend of Good Women*, in Benson, *RC*, 620–24.

4. On the ideology of "the one and only," see Klaus Theweleite, *Male Fantasies*, trans. Stephen Conway, 2 vols. (Minneapolis: University of Minnesota Press, 1987), 1:325–31.

5. Richard Strauss, *Ariadne auf Naxos*, libretto by Hugo von Hofmannsthal, trans. Peggie Cochrane (London: Decca Record Co., 1979), from the recording conducted by James Levine, Deutsche Grammaphon (Hamburg: Polydor International, 1986), 127, 137, 143.

6. McAlpine, *The Genre of "Troilus and Criseyde*," 186.

7. See Aers, *Chaucer, Langland*, 133, where he comments on the "uncritical nature of her ideology."

8. See Benson, *Chaucer's "Troilus and Criseyde*," 107–8, for a survey of views on the poet's treatment of Criseyde's speech.

9. On "the one and only," see Irigaray, *This Sex Which Is Not One*, 31–32.

10. For Butler's discussion of Irigaray and the "masculinist signifying economy," see Judith Butler, *Gender Trouble* (New York: Routledge, 1990), 9–19 (quotation from 13).

11. Dinshaw, *Chaucer's Sexual Poetics*, 51.

selected bibliography

PRIMARY WORKS

Baugh, A. C., ed. *Chaucer's Major Poetry.* New York: Appleton-Century-Crofts, 1963.

Benson, Larry D., ed. *The Riverside Chaucer.* Boston: Houghton Mifflin, 1987.

Boethius. *The Consolation of Philosophy.* Translated by Richard Green. Indianapolis: Bobbs-Merrill, 1967.

Fisher, John H., ed. *The Complete Poetry and Prose of Geoffrey Chaucer.* New York: Holt, Rinehart, & Winston, 1977.

Henryson, Robert. *The Testament of Cresseid.* Edited by Denton Fox. London: Thomas Nelson & Sons, 1968.

Macrobius. *The Commentary on the Dream of Scipio.* Translated by William Harris Stahl. New York: Columbia University Press, 1952.

Robinson, F. N., ed. *The Works of Geoffrey Chaucer.* 2d ed. Boston: Houghton Mifflin, 1957.

Root, Robert K., ed. *The Book of Troilus and Criseyde by Geoffrey Chaucer.* Princeton, N.J.: Princeton University Press, 1926.

Shoaf, R. A., ed. *Troilus and Criseyde.* East Lansing, Mich.: Colleagues Press, 1989.

Windeatt, Barry A., ed. *Chaucer's "Troilus and Criseyde."* London: Longman's, 1984.

SECONDARY WORKS

Aers, David. *Chaucer, Langland, and the Creative Imagination.* London: Routledge & Kegan Paul, 1980. An astute analysis of the social meaning of Chaucer's poetry, with important comparisons between Chaucer and Langland.

Benson, C. David. *Chaucer's "Troilus and Criseyde."* London: Unwin Hyman, 1990. A thorough guide to major traditions informing *Troilus and Criseyde,* but perhaps too eager to square contemporary perspectives with traditional critical views.

Boitani, Piero, ed. *Chaucer and the Italian Trecento.* Cambridge: Cambridge University Press, 1983. A collection of essays setting Chaucer in the Italian literary context contemporary with him.

Boitani, Piero, and Jill Mann, eds. *The Cambridge Chaucer Companion.* Cambridge: Cambridge University Press, 1986. A strong all-around introduction to many aspects of Chaucer's achievement.

Diamond, Arlyn. "Troilus and Criseyde: The Politics of Love." In *Chaucer in the Eighties,* edited by Julian N. Wasserman and Robert J. Blanch, 93–103. Syracuse, N.Y.: Syracuse University Press, 1986. A compact, astute reading of the poem's sexual politics and power structures.

Dinshaw, Carolyn. *Chaucer's Sexual Poetics.* Madison: University of Wisconsin Press, 1989. A powerful, absolutely contemporary feminist reading of several texts, including *Troilus and Criseyde,* written with wit and verve.

Jordan, Robert. *Chaucer and the Shape of Creation.* Cambridge: Harvard University Press, 1967. An elegant analysis of the poem's compositional structure and its relation to architectural form and thought.

Knight, Stephen. "Chaucer and the Sociology of Literature." *Studies in the Age of Chaucer* 2 (1980): 15–51. A discussion of Chaucer criticism that connects it to other disciplines concerned with social and political organization and that surveys the history of socioliterary criticism.

McAlpine, Monica. *The Genre of "Troilus and Criseyde."* Ithaca, N.Y.: Cornell University Press, 1978. A highly successful analysis of the poem's use of tragic and romance conventions.

Middleton, Anne. "The Idea of Public Poetry in the Reign of Richard II." *Speculum* 53 (1978): 94–114. Compares Chaucer with contemporary English poets to determine his place in the political and literary spheres.

Minnis, A. J. *Chaucer and Pagan Antiquity.* Chaucer Studies, No. 8. Cambridge, England: D. S. Brewer, 1982. A study of how classical, literary, and rhetorical traditions shaped Chaucer's ideas of the pagan world.

Patterson, Lee. *Chaucer and the Subject of History.* Madison: University of Wisconsin Press, 1991. A rich discussion that relates Chaucer's vision of history to subjectivity and social analysis, with a long section on *Troilus and Criseyde.*

Pearsall, Derek. *The Canterbury Tales.* London: George Allen & Unwin, 1985. One of the best discussions of the *Tales* written; detailed discussions of critical traditions are useful in work with *Troilus and Criseyde.*

Pope, Rob. *How to Study Chaucer.* London: Macmillan Education, 1988. A short and snappy guide for British students, with practical suggestions for essays and a healthy skepticism.

Ruggiers, Paul G., ed. *Editing Chaucer: The Great Tradition.* Norman, Okla.: Pilgrim Books, 1984. A collection of excellent essays analyzing the editorial history of Chaucer's works.

Salu, Mary, ed. *Essays on "Troilus and Criseyde."* Cambridge, England: D. S. Brewer, 1979; reprint, 1982. A collection of essays addressing and updating many of the major critical controversies concerning the poem.

Shepherd, G. T. "Troilus and Criseyde." In *Chaucer and Chaucerians*, edited by D. S. Brewer, 65–87. University, Ala.: University of Alabama Press, 1966. A sustained, lucid analysis of the text, managed without reference to critical or scholarly traditions.

Spurgeon, Caroline F. E. *Five Hundred Years of Chaucer Criticism and Allusion, 1357–1900.* 3 vols. Cambridge: Cambridge University Press, 1925; reprint, New York: Russell and Russell, 1960. The standard reference guide for the study of Chaucerian reception.

Stevens, Martin. "The Winds of Fortune in the *Troilus.*" *Chaucer Review* 13 (1979): 285–307. A model article; an analysis of nautical metaphors and their philosophical connections.

Strohm, Paul. *Social Chaucer.* Cambridge: Harvard University Press, 1989. A readable, informative analysis of Chaucer's political context, with attentive readings of major texts, including *Troilus and Criseyde.*

Tatlock, J. S. P., and Arthur G. Kennedy. *A Concordance to the Complete Works of Geoffrey Chaucer*, 1927. Reprint, Gloucester, Mass.: Peter Smith, 1963. An indispensable reference for studies of Chaucer's lexical habits.

Wallace, David. "Chaucer's Continental Inheritance: The Early Poems and *Troilus and Criseyde.*" In *The Cambridge Chaucer Companion*, edited by Piero Boitani and Jill Mann, 19–37. Cambridge: Cambridge University Press, 1986. A fresh and lively introduction to Chaucer's relation to French and Italian traditions.

Wetherbee, Winthrop. *Chaucer and the Poets: An Essay on "Troilus and Criseyde."* Ithaca, N.Y.: Cornell University Press, 1984. Concentrates on Latin, Italian, and French literary allusions in the poem, and on Chaucer's debt to the tradition of the classical *poetae.*

index

155

Index

Somnium Scipionis. See Cicero
Soul, flight of, 104, 108–9, 111,
113, 125, 128–29
Speght, Thomas, 17–18, 20, 23
Spenser, Edmund, 16
Spurgeon, Caroline F. E., 14–25
passim
Statius, 128; *The Thebiad,* 67
Stow, John, 16–18
Strauss, Richard: *Ariadne auf
Naxos,* 133–34, 139
Strode, Ralph, 131
Strohm, Paul, 5
Subjectivity, 32–34, 37–38, 66, 88,
89, 145n6
Symbolic systems, 36–42, 44–45,
51–53, 58, 83–84

Testament of Cresseid. See Henryson, Robert
Thebes, siege of, 67
Three estates. *See* Trifunctional
model

Thynne, Francis, 18
Thynne, William, 16–17, 18
Tresilian, Robert, 4
Trifunctional model (three estates),
40–41
Troy, medieval significance of (New
Troy), 6–7, 10–11, 33, 39,
49–50
Tyrwhitt, Thomas, 20–21

Urry, John, 20–21
Usk, Thomas, 4

Walton, William, 133
Waswo, Richard, 129
Windeatt, Barry A., 15, 20–21
Women, in symbolic systems,
39–40, 45, 51–53, 60, 74, 81,
103, 106, 107, 110, 111–12,
127, 135–37
Wright, Herbert G., 24
Wyatt, Sir Thomas, 23

the author

Allen J. Frantzen teaches Old and Middle English literature at Loyola University of Chicago. He is the author of *The Literature of Penance in Anglo-Saxon England* (1983), *King Alfred* (1986), and *Desire for Origins: New Language, Old English, and Teaching the Tradition* (1990) and editor of *Speaking Two Languages: Tradition and Contemporary Theory in Medieval Studies* (1991).